"By wisdom a house is built, and through understanding it is established,"

Proverbs 24:3.

The Overcomer's Toolkit ISBN: 978-0-9895057-4-1 © 2016 by Sunday Dieke

PRINTED IN THE UNITED STATES OF AMERICA

Table of Contents

Acknowledgments

I am very grateful to the following for making this book a reality:

My darling wife, *Ngozi*, for her love, encouragement, ideas, suggestions and constructive feedback.

The benevolent *Pastor Benson Agbortogo* for his invaluable help and support.

Dr. Jon Crook for his expert feedback and sensible editing that helped produce a masterpiece of clarity and brevity.

Ms. Paulette Hollingsworth for editing the initial draft of this book.

Mr. Paul Nyamweya for helping with technical editing.

My mentors and teachers alike for the impartation of their ideas into this book.

Dr. Mike Murdock for encouraging us, his partners, to write about our persuasions.

Mr. & Mrs. Ngozi Onwuzurumba for their generosity and support.

My amazing children: *Armstrong, Josiah, Praise & Levi* for their love, patience and forbearance.

And the following members of my family for their prayers and support: My lovely mom, *Esther Ogbonne Nwankolo Dieke*; my mother-in-law, *Sarah Okolo*; and my siblings: *Bridgette, Frank, Ann,* and *Vera*; as well as *Felicia* and *Basil*.

About This Book

Emotional turmoil and distress should never *enslave you!*

These are adversarial weapons that can *prevent* you from *fulfilling* your God-given dreams and goals.

This book focuses on a Christian believer's *typical* experiences and the adversaries he or she might encounter in life. It is a clarion call to *winning* spiritual warfare. It will *awaken* the dormant areas of your life, *sharpen* your sensitivity and give you the tools to *overcome* spiritual and emotional adversarial forces.

This book was specifically designed for you if you are feeling *hopeless, helpless, alone* or *confused* as you encounter life's many challenges and storms.

You will be *inspired* and *equipped* with the tools to *overcome.*

Why I Wrote This Book

You do not have to accept a life of failure.

Many give up hope and *abandon* their dreams and goals when life's problems seem *insurmountable*. Some sever ties with God and inadvertently *surrender* to the power of the enemy; which is the *chief* driver of catastrophic events in their life. This is a very troubling trend to observe; because I know, from the depths of my heart, that solutions are within reach...*just unrecognized.*

The answer is not *hidden* in some *abstract* formula or in a person with *mysterious* powers, but in something God has already made *available* to us; because He knew we would encounter storms in life.

The ultimate question remains, what do you do when life takes an *unexpected* turn? There will be times when it seems you have fallen into life's dangerous pit and do not know how to get out of it. The good news is...*there is a way out.* That is precisely what this book is *designed* to help you discover.

You will need an *arsenal* of weapons and a toolkit with *specific* tools.

I wrote this book out of my own experiences. As one who has encountered turbulence in my own life, I wrote this to show *you* that the power of faith can *triumph* in a world of secular reality. I share certain Biblical principles and techniques that have helped me triumph over *adversarial* forces and *dark* seasons.

I believe that you too can overcome by adopting the same principles contained in this book.

Introduction

The Christian life is a philosophy.

Some people believe that giving their life to Christ *shields* them from every conceivable tragedy and adversity on the face of the earth. That is not the case. Life on earth bears its own challenges to *everyone*, including believers and non-believers alike.

Hardship does not *ask* for permission to schedule itself on your calendar. Jesus *faced* it. His own disciples did too. The Apostle Paul had a great *encounter* with God, yet he spent *most* of his life in *prison*, despite the fact that he was living *righteously*.

As you can easily see, *temptation* and *adversity* have befallen men since Creation. They are the *uninvited* guests who will show up at your party, whether you are prepared to host them or not. You do not have to accommodate or entertain them, but you can *resist* and *deter* them. To do so effectively, you will need to understand how to engage in combat...*the art of spiritual warfare.*

Choosing to live for Christ is the *wisest* decision you will ever make in your lifetime. It *guarantees* eternal life in paradise, but it requires much *preparation* while you are still living on the earth. Your experience of life here on earth will be both *enjoyable* and *unpleasant*. At times, it will even be *unpredictable;* but you can live *prepared*. Since adversity is *inevitable*, you can live *ready* to overcome.

For this simple reason...*life is warfare!*

Calamities often strike *without* prior warning, and you probably never have sufficient time to *adequately* prepare. There-fore, it makes sense to *invest* time in mastering the art of warfare against the *inevitable* dark seasons of your life...*before they are upon you.*

What Is...A Dark Season?

A dark season could be a "power outage" of the mind that oftentimes creeps up on you *stealthily*. A dark season is usually accompanied by trial, temptation, failure, despondency and a general lack of inspiration. Dark seasons seem *unending*. A dark season is more of a *feeling* than it is a place. You experience an *intense* feeling of *despair* and *discouragement* because of the *avalanche* of perturbing life events you are *battered* with.

Any illumination within you is *quenched* like a sudden power outage. Your daylight *disappears*. Your whole world turns into the stark darkness of night. A darkness that seems to stay *indefinitely*; with dawn nowhere in sight. Things may appear *normal* on the outside to a casual, unsuspecting observer; *but on the inside your world is falling apart*. Others cannot sense how *fragmented* your life has become. Yet, you know deep inside, that everything is going dead wrong. You feel *stripped* of every iota of joy and happiness.

This dark passage in your life-journey has evolved into a season of *drought*; loaded with a *relentless* slew of *undesirable* and *endless* outcomes and occurrences.

Does This Sound Familiar?

Your Seeds do not seem to produce any *desired* Harvests.

Every effort to repair and rebuild seems *inconsequential*. Unconsciously, you begin to *develop* and *nurture* negative thoughts. You embark on a journey through your memories. You find yourself *camped* on Hurt & Disappointment Avenue. All it does is *feed* and *sustain* a cycle of negative thoughts; no matter how positive you *purpose* to be.

People around you do not usually notice anything major that could be wrong with you. In fact, some think the exact *opposite*; "that you are living your best life now." Every step *toward* a remedy seems like a move in a *contrary* direction.

Your *cheerfulness* and *joy*...is *short-lived*.

Your *patience*...stretches *thin*.

Your *will* to live...*wanes*.

Unbeknownst to many, you might even be considering placing yourself on *suicide watch*.

God seems to be a million miles *away*. You proclaim The Word of The Living God over your circumstances; but it seems *lifeless* or *ineffectual* in creating any impactful change. You can still sense the *potency* of God's Word; just not in your particular situation or predicament.

You may be financially...*broke*.

You may be spiritually...*impotent*.

You may be socially...*bankrupt*.

You may be physically...*exhausted*.

Your motivation has slowly but surely *disappeared* as you hit "rock-bottom." Many negative events may have *loomed* as your life took unexpected turns.

Items in your home may begin to break down *suddenly*, and at the wrong time too. All the things you cannot do without.

Vehicles.

Refrigerators.

Air conditioning units (during a hot Texas summer)!

Everything from major to minor appliances. As one handyman leaves another is on the way. An invisible, destructive spirit seems to be at work, *wrecking* your world and causing untold *damage*.

Your health or the health of those under your care may start *failing* in some minor or even major ways. You are now having to make *frequent* trips to the doctor.

Just as The Bible describes blessings overtaking the righteous; during such tumult, misfortune seems to be *dominating* your life. It appears as if a *curse* has come upon your life. You suspect there must be some strange, invisible force or an archenemy at work...and sadly, *that enemy is now in your backyard*. You whisper to yourself that "this could be anything but a random act." Finally, you come to the conclusion that there must be *a snake in your garden*.

Questions begin to *explode*. You flood yourself with double barrel questions: "What have I done and what should I do?" You seek revelation from God, but it is not forthcoming; and if at all, not as *fast* as you would like. You look to the left and to the right for answers...*but to no avail*.

You go to church on Sundays, vying for the front seat, hoping to receive a "special word" from your pastor...*but nothing happens*. You go to sleep, looking forward to a meaningful dream...*but the night bears no message*. If you dream at all, it is quickly forgotten...*long before dawn*. If you are lucky enough to remember any of your dreams...*they cannot be deciphered*. Your attempts at fasting are ineffective...*oftentimes without encouraging results*.

Your problems seem to *defy* all logic.

You *retreat* into solitude and *degenerate* into deep pondering. You arrive at the *hasty* conclusion that no one cares about you; "that you could die today and nobody would even pause to acknowledge your life!"

You undertake a *quick*, but *careful*, examination of your mind to make sure you are not crazy. Of course, you can still *reason* and *think* correctly. You reassure yourself that you are mentally sound, since you are well-oriented to your surroundings and circumstances. After all, you are still able to formulate good ideas about what you want to do...*except you do not seem able to implement or execute any.*

Your hope is fading...*fast.*

You feel like you are stalling...*lifeless.*

Your ability to focus has become harder...*fragmented.*

You nudge yourself awake, but the *devil* reminds you that your previous efforts did not gain any ground. It seems like armed guardsmen are standing in your way...*between you and your cherished dreams.* Your past successes are now nothing to write home about.

You scan every possible angle of your life. You are unable to discern any major thing that you are doing wrong. Only *one* thing stands out. *All you are getting is bad results.* You take a tour of your recent and early life, searching for where you could have sinned; *withheld* The Tithe, *offended* God or other people.

The more you look the less you see!

On the contrary, you might even get cocky, believing that *you* are holy. After all, you could not spot any major sin in your life that could be a potential *magnet* for the high level of disappointment and agony that has befallen you. Then you ask, "Where are you God?" You do this as *odd competes with even...un-*

*certainty persists…*in an *endless, fierce, noiseless battle* that seems to rage on *forever.* Yet, again and again, *you* are the casualty.

However, if you happen to recall an apparent character *flaw* or *weakness* you are struggling with, you begin to nurture *doubt* as to whether God *truly* forgave you of your sins. You conclude that payback time for the wrongs of your life has finally arrived. "Maybe karma is real." You degenerate into *destructive introspection.* You make the *hasty* conclusion that "God is subjecting you to the power of the enemy." This kind of *paralyzing* mind-battle can go on for an *unspecified* length of time.

What Do You Do…Next?

What do you do when you find yourself in a situation like this? When your world is *falling apart* and your solutions are *not working.* When your will to live is *diminishing* and your determination to fight *ebbing.* When your experience with God is different from the God-experience you read or hear others talk about. When you cannot accurately *explain* your situation to another. When you lack the right words to *express* your anxiety. When you wish your *honest* response to every "how are you?" question would truly be "fine" even though all was not well with you. You *mechanically* answer "fine" because you lack the confidence that the person asking could administer any real healing or solution.

What do you do when you retire each night wishing you do not have to wake up to the next morning, but you do anyway? When you see *no hope* for your dreams and goals. When your brook has *dried up,* but you have not yet discovered your next instruction from God. When every door you knock on seems to turn into a *brick wall.* When your wish for each new day to signal an *end* to your problem is dashed again and again. When the things you *dread the most* seem to occupy your thoughts and mind. When it seems God is a *Spectator* to your struggles and not your Ally. When life no longer has meaning and you feel all *alone* in your struggles...or so it seems. *So, what do you do?*

You need to know what to do next...*and you cannot afford to be wrong.* The world will throw junk at you, in your face and from behind. You can only do one of two things: *give up...or fight to the finish.*

Do you oftentimes wish you could take care of your enemies with a fist fight or even a physical weapon? But you know, "it is not a fight against flesh and blood but against principalities and evil powers." (Ephesians 6). As a believer, you have something *more powerful* than any form of firepower or natural weapons.

You have The Word of God.

Your *biggest* problem may be the lack of a proper *understanding* of the weapons at your disposal and how to properly *deploy* them, as opposed to not having any. So, how can you *exit* this "dangerous pit" you find yourself in?

Lose hope...*accepting* the status quo?

Pray...*wishing* your enemy would stop or have pity on you?

Retreat...*assuming* the trouble will die with time?

Resign...*hoping* God will take care of the problem?

Or should you *learn* new strategies and techniques to *fight* until you conquer and overcome? It is not a question of whether the enemy will *cease his attacks,* because he will not. It is more the uncertainty of *when* and *how* he will declare *more* wars against you. You can prepare to fight back instead of being a silent victim...*doing nothing and waiting endlessly on God.* Stories of those who waited ignorantly on God do not always end quite well.

You Will Pass Through Adversity

Hardly anyone goes through life without passing through *tumultuous* times. I have had my fair share of adversity. I have endured seasons of *rejection*. It was certainly not because of a bad attitude or a major character flaw on my part. *A peculiar season of darkness had come upon me.*

Every prospective business or social contact I tried to establish was downright unsuccessful, no matter how hard I tried! At the onset, things usually started out great. The other party exuded enthusiasm until I tried to advance the relationship or initiated efforts to take things to the next level.

Suddenly, things would take an *unexpected* turn and the outcome was almost always *unsavory*. To say that this was frustrating is to state the obvious. I would bombard myself with questions and self-talks. "This same person I had just spoken to, who showed a high level of interest and admiration, suddenly reneged! What could have possibly changed their mind? What did I do wrong?"

Such events left me bewildered and paralyzed. I often wondered if I was a *ghost* in my own skin. What could possibly *erase* every positive impression about me from the memory of those I was trying to establish a relationship with? That by itself was a morale killer.

Did This Really Happen To Me?

I have experienced war and combat as a soldier. Yet, nothing can be more *scary* and *excruciating* as the conflict that can occur in a person's mind. I am not talking about mental illness or any physical or emotional abnormality; but about the "war within." A *raging* mind battle, that includes the visible and invisi-

14

ble forces directed against you, which hell manipulates to keep you *defeated*.

I have encountered seasons of hardship, both *simultaneously* and in *succession*. I even share a few of them in this book. However, the good news is, God's Word *never* failed during such *turbulent* times!

I got married *late* in life. Shortly after tying the knot, my wife and I decided to have kids as *quickly* as God could give them to us. Unfortunately, conception did not happen as swiftly as we had both anticipated. That raised the suspicion that something was *wrong*. We did what every sensible couple does; rule out any medical condition.

Sure enough we encountered some roadblocks, which we dealt with expeditiously; *but still no conception!* That's when it became clear that we were facing an uphill battle. We sowed *warfare* seeds. We contacted as many intercessors as we knew to join forces in *Prayer* on our behalf. I still vividly remember my wife asking God to "fill our house with the noises of children..."

Well, the results of such requests were *three* babies in four years, plus the *fourth* baby eight years later. Our home has since been *filled* with not only "noises" but with the sounds of *celebration*. While sitting in the comfort of my own home, I sometimes wonder if am in a stadium! The plea has since then *changed* from "let there be noises" to "can all be quiet" or "talk one more time and see...what brand of mom those noises can produce" as *a sweet mother becomes a strict disciplinarian.*

After we had our second child, Josiah, we felt like we were done having children. But then our third baby, Praise, came along and we were like, "God you've really blessed us enough..."

Then my wife found out she was pregnant again with our fourth baby, Levi (The High Priest). It then became obvious that only God could *stop* such immaculate conceptions!

As you can see, the erstwhile couple who longed for *more* kids have suddenly turned into activists for population *control*. So, one day in our local Church, my wife ran into one of our Holy Ghost-filled Pastors who *interceded* for us during the *drought* season and told him; "Hello Pastor Holton, I would like for you to reverse that prayer you prayed for us (years ago) to have children. We have more than enough now but they keep coming..."

Just before the bewildered pastor could utter a word, his lovely wife intervened, "No, Mrs. Ngozi, I think you should go to the doctor..." Everyone present burst into laughter! The lesson here is to be *mindful* what you pray for. By the way, we love each of our children. We remain *thankful* to God for blessing us with such *marvelous* children.

I have had seasons when it seemed the enemy tried to *block* our streams of income in an attempt to *strip* my family of our joy. But our joy comes from The Lord, not from a *person* or a *thing*. Despite being *astute* in faith, my wife and I have encountered rough times in areas and ways we *least* expected. The "coalition of the angry" cooked up whooping lies against us.

My wife and I are of African descent. We have had people in my life who have taken our names and pictures to devilish shrines, witchdoctors and the like, in an attempt to *dismantle* our marriage and *stop* us from procreating. All their efforts are null and void because we remain under the *protection* and *abiding grace* of The Most High God.

Life After The Army

In January 2008, I left the U.S. Army to explore a career with a private oil firm. By April of the following year, barely a year into the new job, the wind of layoffs was blowing strong. I referred to it as the equivalent of a Category 5 hurricane. My wife was almost three months pregnant with our first son, Armstrong. Week after week, employees were let go in succession, because of the so called *glut* in the oil industry. Anxiety levels *skyrocketed* among those of us who were still left standing, even though they rest assured us that our jobs will be *safe* and *secure*.

On the morning of April 15, 2009, I was summoned along with four or five others, including my erstwhile boss, who had *pacified* us by telling us that we would *not* be affected. The "breaking news" was heart-wrenching, reading like a familiar headline: "Sorry, you have lost your job…!"

Suddenly, an urgent and dire need to find another job swept through me like a cold breeze passing through the night. It seemed my trouble had just begun. That next job was nowhere on the radar! Every attempt at finding one was *unsuccessful* as the days turned into weeks and the weeks into months. It got to a point where I felt "overqualified" in applying for any entry level job out there since "the right ones" had nothing in store for me. The more places I applied to, the more *rejections* I encountered.

After several failures, my self-esteem began to *shrink* as quickly as a deflating tire on a highway. I was becoming *weak* inside without much energy or motivation. Any new efforts only seemed to ask for the obvious; *more failure and rejection.*

It didn't seem like I was doing anything right. But in hindsight, I knew for sure I did certain things *right*. I stayed *very close* to God. He was my place of *solitude*, so I retreated to Him often. My local church was a place of *inspiration*, so I stayed close to it too. I labored to keep some relationships *alive*, especially the ones that *steered* me toward God; despite the temptation to *withdraw* into my shell, while under self-imposed solitary confinement.

God Did It Before!

I had to remind myself of how God *rallied* to help me in the past. Of particular interest was an incident in 1999, shortly after I immigrated to the U.S. from Nigeria. I was in *desperate* need for a part-time job but could not find the right fit. Day after day, I felt like a hungry lion in the midst of deer and antelope, yet *unable* to make a kill. I began to nurse a punishing sense of guilt for not achieving any results on something as prosaic as finding a part-time job.

One day I made a decision to walk into *every* business establishment along a major street in Beaumont, Texas, and to ask if they had any job opening or needed some help, without *regard* to their line of business. One particular shop I walked into had *strange* and *unfamiliar* equipment on display. I politely introduced myself to the two young men inside. Before I turned to leave, they burst into laughter. To this day, I do not know why they were laughing so hard. It is possible they thought I was lost or misguided for venturing into an "odd" place to ask for a job. I suspect they tossed out my resume as quickly as I turned to leave. Their laughter and rejection did not deter me. I continued my search until I had gone into every other business place as planned.

To cut a long story short, all those seemingly gigantic efforts did not yield any dividends, since I did not get invited back to a single job interview. However, a week or two later, I received a call from an unrelated source. A friend heard that I was looking for a job and called to offer me an opportunity at a pharmaceutical company. It happened to be a *delightful* work experience. I *enjoyed* every aspect of the job, including my schedule, coworkers and our customers alike.

The Power of Your Memory

The memory of such a past victory became instrumental for *resuscitating* my downright collapsed *inspiration system*. I refused to give up hope, but continued *asking, seeking* and *believing*; because "if God did it before He will do it again." From that past experience, I summoned the *courage* to keep swimming *against* the currents while maintaining my *faith* in God.

I would not be telling the truth if I pretended that being jobless was any less nerve-racking for me than, say, watching a scary movie. Nothing was more agonizing than being constantly bombarded with the thought that my family had *no* income at a time when we needed it the *most*. To make matters worse, it seemed as if all our *monthly* bills were due on a *weekly* basis. That is the reality for the one without a job, with plenty of bills to pay.

My wife's pregnancy was becoming *visible* with each passing day; a stark reminder that our new baby, Armstrong, would soon be ushered into this world. The unsettling truth was that he may arrive at a time when dad was jobless! I *considered* filing for unemployment benefits as much as I hated doing so; but I believe there was an inner prompting that *discouraged* me from doing so. *I heeded*.

The Birthing of A Prayer Ministry

As the dark season persisted; I asked myself the ultimate question: "What should I do?" My wife and I waged a *unified* crusade; we fought back at our common problems instead of fighting each other. We cried out to God *together*. We were healed *simultaneously*. We *comforted* each other by being emotionally *available* for each other.

We *solidified* our Prayer Life. We learned to pray with powerful *authority* and *unwavering* faith in God like never before. Guess what? New Prayer Warriors were birthed.

Out of this experience...we became intercessors!

Out of nowhere, friends and family alike were *asking* us to pray for *them*, unlike anything we had ever seen before. The more we prayed for others, the more great testimonies came to us that God answered through *our* prayers. If you do not stay aware of God's *involvement*, nothing can be more egotistical!

Through that experience we learned to stand *firmly* on The Word of God and to remind Him about His promises as contained in the scriptures. We oftentimes *remind* God that He promised "not to abandon nor forsake us" and frankly, He hasn't. We remind Him that He promised "to grant the desires of the upright," and our needs have never gone *unmet*. We cry out to Him by *pleading* The Blood of Jesus on a *daily* basis over every area of our lives. The Blood was not shed in *vain*, and we have never ran *out* of solutions!

We reached out to intercessors who joined forces in *declaring* God's Word on our behalf. He had answered *us* when we prayed for *others*. We knew He would *answer* when others in turn prayed for us...and that is exactly how it has been.

We believed what God says instead of what people say and that has become our *guiding* principle. We remind God what He said in Deuteronomy 28:7; *"Your enemy shall come one way but flee in seven"* and that is what has been happening for us.

After five months of unemployment, I was mentally depleted from the *endless* job hunt. Then one day, there seemed to be a light at the end of the tunnel. I received invitations to two different job interviews just days apart. On my way to one of the interviews, I stopped at my local bank to withdraw some cash.

God Can Get A Word To You...Even At The Bank

A *friendly* cashier asked, "What type of job do you do?"

I replied, "I do not have one right now, but am looking."

Without hesitation, she proclaimed, "Today you will have a job." *Just like that!* I had never disclosed to her or anyone else in that bank that I was headed for a job interview that morning. But, just like that, she "prophesied."

Out of that interview, I got hired as a probation officer by The Tarrant County Community Supervision and Correction Department (CSCD). I am still working with them today.

A few weeks after I started working, I received a call from my former employer, the oil firm, asking if I would come back to work for them. Without hesitation, my response was, "No, but thank you!"

I turned it down, not because I was grieved, but because I knew it was not the *right* place for me. After all, the only reason I ventured into the oil sector was because it was supposed to be *lucrative*. The job itself was not motivating. The constant travel it required *robbed* me of time with God and my family.

God Will Get A Message To You...Early

At some point in my crisis, I remembered a dream I had while preparing to disengage from the military. It was a dream *warning* about the potential dangers ahead. In hindsight, that strange dream made sense, but I did not *heed* the caution. That was due to my lack of understanding and failure to seek wise counsel. You see, God will always *warn* you about potential dangers ahead in one way or another; but it is up to you to *discern* and *obey*, or *disregard* His warnings and instructions.

I could tell you one life story after another about God's unique ways of intervention in my personal life. How do I know it was God and not probability or chance? There was always something *personal* and *remarkable* that proved to me it was God and not a coincidence or a mere chance.

My marriage could have *ended* as quickly as it started. It could have ended like a *first round knockout* in a heavyweight boxing bout. But "what God put together, let no man try to put asunder." (See Matthew 19:6.) Thanks be to God that both my wife and I understood the nature of the problems we faced. We learned early enough to *trust* in God and to fight *together* as opposed to fighting each other. Otherwise, it would have long been over.

Knowing God made a huge difference for us. It enabled us to get back together *after* each fight; just like a team that *loses* a game but realizes they would soon be playing again. Even when differences revolved around our approach to child rearing, we labored to *stick together* in the midst of disagreement. We unofficially earned ourselves the title of "crusader couple."

The principle of fighting *together* instead of against each other was a win-win for our family; only because God is the *common* denominator in everything we do. We placed God at the *center* of every blessing, problem or obstacle by believing strongly that solutions come through His Word.

My Marriage Has Been Tested!

My marriage has passed through the furnace and been engrossed by fire. Our journey together as husband and wife was once like an obstacle course: strenuous, enduring, excruciating and painful. But at the same time, it was *peaceful*. Peaceful because, as I have said, God is The Cornerstone of our foundation and we learned not to fight each other but *united* against our common enemies.

There were times when every step along the way seemed like a baby-step in an *endless* journey through a dangerous minefield. It was a journey indeed; one without end through *unfamiliar* terrain. But not any more, since we learned the potent weapons inherent in The Word of The Living God. We fought back the darkness by keeping the flame *alive* through The Word of The Living God, and by the power of The Holy Spirit.

The bottom line is that the Christian believer's life is not a nest without thorns. There can be difficult challenges along the way. At times you must navigate the strangest experiences that you would not even wish on your worst enemy. But, when the darkness erupts the Light of God will *always* thrive!

> *The Christian life is not a nest without thorns.*

When Darkness Erupts

What do you do when the "darkness" erupts?

An overcomer should *know* what to do; what works and what does not. I knew the difference in the outcome when I *waited on* God versus when I *worked with* God.

The Bible is the most popular book in history. In many countries, it is *easily* accessible too; yet very few *truly* grasp its content. In it are open, yet *hidden* secrets; hidden in the sense that very *few* people know *how* to work them! More often than not, our understanding of The Bible is intellectual instead of *experiential* or through *revelation* from The Holy Spirit.

Many can read it, but very *few* study it.

Among those who *study* The Bible, only a *small* percentage really know how to *apply* it. To the majority out there, it is just another document of history. Not all who say they *believe* it actually *do* what it says. How can you believe and not obey? The Bible is a testament of God's will and as believers we *share* in that will. We have to *believe* what God says and *declare* what God promises.

As you read on you will begin to discover some of the Biblical truths that will help *unlock* you. The techniques may not be new to a *seasoned* believer, but their efficacies are so profound. They must not escape from your memory, whether you are new and growing or advanced in faith; because life is full of potentially rugged and treacherous terrain which you must journey through each hour of your existence while here on the earth.

You will need a tool box with certain *indispensable* tools.

Things in your world will break down and they will need to be *fixed*. Every now and then your "life-sink" will *clog*. If it is not unclogged, life will *stink!*

You may feel you need *more* than what I have shared in this book, but I guarantee that for an *overcoming* life you cannot do *without* the things I have shared thus far. I have also discussed auxiliary issues that, at face value, may seem to have no direct bearing on the subject, but they are part of the *equation* for an overcoming life. These are *hygiene matters*, if you would.

For example, your *attitude* towards a man of God makes a world of difference, especially when you are facing challenges of a *spiritual* nature. You may ponder the relationship between your *opinion* of a man of God and leading an *overcoming* life. You will always *need* a man of God in your life in one way or another.

Remember, what you condemn...you cannot attract.

Positive *thinking* and the right *attitude* towards people can also make a world of difference during your seasons of affliction. You will *need* other people. You cannot work with the people you *despise.*

I hope this book will be both *useful* and *interesting* at the same time, *equipping* you with the tools to overcome so you can begin to live a more *fulfilling* life.

Chapter 1

The 9 Irreplaceable Elements of Your Life-Journey

1. The Holy Spirit

Jesus *promised* The Holy Spirit to His disciples; who were *troubled* by His impending departure following The Resurrection. He then promised to *send* them a Comforter and He surely *fulfilled* that promise.

John 14:26; *"But The Advocate, The Holy Spirit, Whom The Father will send in My Name, will teach you all things and remind you of everything I have said to you."*

You will need the Holy Spirit as your Source of Light and Mentorship. Without light, it will be difficult to *see* and *navigate* through the dark alleys of life. Without guidance, you would be *lost*.

2. People

You will need relationships with people. You will need some people to come *into* your life and others to *exit* from it. You will need *trusted* Godly persons such as mentors and intercessors who can give you *wise* counsel. These are the ones who will join forces with you in Prayer, to pray the same prayers as you would pray for yourself. Continuously ask The Holy Spirit to *connect* you with right kind of people, and learn to nurture right relationships.

3. The Word

You will need The Word of God as your *blueprint* and *guide* to living. The Word of God contains hidden *solutions* to all human problems and those that have mastered it have *mastered* life. Most importantly, The Word is your *principal* weapon. The scripture rightly points out in Ephesians 6:17 that The Word is **"The Sword of The Spirit."** You will need to *constantly proclaim* The Word as you wage warfare.

4. Inspiration

You need a *constant source* of encouragement from your-self and possibly others, if you are to overcome the dangerous obstacles that lie ahead in your journey. As we read in Psalms, King David had to constantly *encourage himself* in The Lord. So, you too will need to be able to encourage *yourself.*

Receiving encouragement from *others* will help as you strive to overcome the many obstacles you may face on your life's journey. Without encouragement or inspiration, there is no *motivation*; which is the *fuel* for your mind. Without motivation there would not be a *sustained concentration*, and without a *focus* there can be no *accomplishment* of your worthwhile goals.

5. Prayer

You need to master how to talk *to God* and how God talks *to you*. Prayer can be to you what an electrode is to a bat-tery. A used up battery is weak…and you would be too if you did not pray *habitually*, *purposefully* and *effectively.*

Throughout history, all overcomers, including Jesus Himself, had *established* prayer routines. In the same light, *you* must pray habitually if you are to overcome.

6. The Power of Love

Love is the most *elevated* of all the virtues and a big part of the equation in your quest for an overcoming life. Apostle Paul said in 1 Cor. 13:13 that *"love is the greatest..."* Jesus talked to His disciples about *"love of their enemies."* Jesus knew you could not conquer in the *absence* of love.

Love is however highly misunderstood. It is not merely the *opposite* of hate as in "the flipping of a coin." You can still *lack* in love without *hating* anyone. Love encompasses the *passion* for righteousness and the *desire* to fulfill your duties and obligations towards God, people and things.

> *Love is not merely the opposite of hate; you could still lack in love without hating anyone.*

7. Prosperity Through Godly Principles

Poverty or destitution can be a *magnifier* of adversity just like abundance or riches can become a *shock absorber* during hard times. The pain of hunger can double when there is no food available at all as opposed to a simple *delay* in your eating schedule.

Money is a *catalyst* for solving problems. Having enough of it helps *lighten* your load during times of trouble. Learn to *attract*, *manage*, and *spend* money wisely. During your season of adversity, you will be glad you did.

8. A Warrior Mentality

Warfare is *inescapable*.

Dr. Mike Brown of Strength and Wisdom Ministries often charges believers to "stop whining and start warring."

You need to develop the *mentality* of a conqueror. The Bible commands in Matthew 18:18 to *"tie and bind evil forces."* A boxer in the ring cannot *win* the fight without throwing jabs and power punches. Somebody once wrote that "life is like riding a bicycle and you fall if you stop pedaling."

You will *lose* the war if you *stop* fighting.

Champions *train* and *fight* to win. An overcoming lifestyle is no different. God does not do the fighting *for* you, He fights *with* you. A pastor issued the challenge, "Can you shout the shout that brings down the wall or do you only shout after the wall has crumbled?" *So, can you shout to bring down your wall?*

9. Mastery of Your Arsenal of Weapons

A soldier is *conversant* and *comfortable* with his weapon system. Develop the *knowledge* and *mastery* of your weapons. Be *aggressive* in deploying them with deadly accuracy and precision. Be knowledgeable of God's Word and declare it *constantly*, *purposefully* and with *conviction*. That is a must for overcoming.

Our Prayer Together

That God may grant you the vision, plan, strategy and strength (VPSS) to overcome the jolting trials and warfare of life as you journey through the obscure and treacherous terrain of your life, in The Name of Jesus.

Chapter 2

Your Life...An Obscure Journey

The Christian life experience is a unique one.

The Christian experience *differs* from one person to another. At one point or other, you are bound to *encounter* "dark times" in your journey of faith. It is a season when your level of faith appears to no longer produce any *desired* results. The foundation of your belief not only becomes shakable, but *questionable* as well. It would appear as if there was a sudden deactivation of your faith control panel into an *inactive* mode. You feel *empty*, all *alone* and *without* influence. You could become engrossed with *doubt*, *confusion* and *fear*.

Just imagine embarking on a long journey:

You pack up your luggage. The weather is clear and bright, your vehicle is trip-ready and you hit the road in typical weather you are accustomed to driving in.

Somewhere along the way, in the middle of nowhere, the weather suddenly changes. Dusk is fast approaching. Visibility becomes poor, the road narrows, and your surroundings are now isolated and dangerously unfamiliar. Mother Nature unleashes a flooding rain. Your windshield wipers suddenly stop working. You begin to slow down. You reach for your cell phone but you have no reception or signal.

You begin to panic, not knowing what to expect next as you are faced with scores of negative possibilities. The nearest place to a motel, gas station or other motorists is a hundred miles away. You call on God; but it seems He is on vacation. Everything you try seems null and void and to no avail. The more you try, the more your world turns against you. You do not know whether to proceed forward, backward or to remain still. You are not sure whether the gas in your tank will sustain you till help arrives or if you are safe from the dangerous wilds.

You ask God why He allowed this to happen to you or even let you embark on this trip in the first place. As you languish in isolation, you panic in fear and confusion.

Your Life…Is A Progression of Seasons

Literally, everyone, believers and non-believers alike, at one point or another, may encounter a season of *desolation* and *drought* such that their predicament may be *similar* to or even *worse* than that of the imaginary sojourner depicted above.

When you face an agonizing situation like this, not only do you become *doubtful* that your prayers are getting answered, but you also become *convinced* that all is well with everyone else; including your next door neighbor, members of your local Church, people you see on the television screen, at the drugstore, or immediately around you.

You become *critical, embittered,* and *reclusive.* You gravitate towards *self-interrogation:* "When did I miss God, and what wrong have I done?"

You may even begin to question God with thoughts like, "Maybe God only responds to some people; God doesn't really care about me."

Satan, whose job is to create fear, confusion, doubt and defeat, continues to wage war *against* you. You may begin to *backslide* in your faith. You may feel like you completely *lost* your mind. Sermons, inspirational songs and the things that used to inspire and minister to you no longer do.

The Word of God seems to have *little* or *no* value to the point you no longer have faith in the scriptures. You do not seem to believe familiar Bible verses that may be *applicable* to your situation. If at all you do meditate on The Word of God, you do not summon enough faith to *activate* it to work for you. You are *tempted* to conclude that The Bible is no longer working for you even though you still believe it is The Word of The Living God.

You feel inwardly *ashamed* for not receiving a certain measure of Blessing commensurate with your *perceived* level of faith. In other words, it seems that you are not living up to certain *mundane* expectations and assume that *everyone* knows this to be true. It becomes self-evident that you are not a recipient of blessings or rewards deserving of one who *truly* serves God. You become *susceptible* to self-comparison and the *blame* game: self-blaming, God-blaming and the blaming of circumstances.

Worse still, your inner conversation or self-talk begins to drift *off course*. You *cage* your faith, your imagination and the ability to converse with The Holy Spirit in a lockbox; with the key long misplaced. You continue to drift into *loss* of hope, a *critical* attitude, and the nursing of *fears*.

Fear is an *uninvited* perilous guest that is not in a hurry to leave once you open the door to it. That mental state is very *deadly*; more dangerous than bullets. It is *poisonous* and manifests in various forms.

3 Fears You Will Encounter

1. The Fear...of Reaching Out

Reaching out is an absolute *necessity* for anyone in a crisis...*whether you are reaching out to God or to other people*. Some of us are *afraid* to reach out to others simply because we do not want them to *misjudge* us. So you resign to *die* in silence!

Your "dark" season will *linger* as long as you *wallow* in fear, *refuse* to seek help, or *resist* opening up to wise, trustworthy and reliable counsel; especially from Godly sources. As long as you dwell in fear, it will begin to take *control* of your life, to *rule* over you and *invite* her other cousins such as depression, isolation and deprivation to join forces against you.

As this drags on, even the most *profound* scriptures seem like mere *statements*, lacking God's Power and Authority. For example, scriptures like these no longer *encourage* you.

Proverbs 15:22; *"That plans fail for lack of counsel, but with advisers they succeed."*

Matthew 18:19; *"If two of you on earth agree about anything you ask for, it will be done for you by My Father in heaven."*

Deuteronomy 32:30; *"One of us can put a thousand to flight but two can put ten thousand to flight."*

Look For The Open Door…Out of Your Crisis

The good news is, the moment you begin to *open up* and *reach out* to trusted ones, you begin to regain the *awareness* that you are *not alone* in your struggles. Reaching out can be direct or indirect. Sometimes just *listening* to sermons, *attending* conferences, *participating* in support groups, or even *reading up* on specific subjects relating to your unique circumstances can open up *new* opportunities into your future or become an *exit* from your crippling situation.

When you are able to connect with someone who can *relate* to your specific situation, who has been *where* you are and experienced *what* you are experiencing, it becomes a *normalizing* experience for you. The question is can you *reach out* to somebody today? Who can you *confide in* that will be a solution rather than *additional* problem?

You most certainly do not need anyone who will *trivialize* your pain, *compromise* your confidentiality or *worsen* your situation. Anyone capable of *betraying* the confidence and trust that you have placed in them cannot be of any real help. Falling into such hands will add salt to your wounds, hence the need to exercise *caution* about who you *trust* and *confide* in, especially during your season of vulnerability. Having said so, you must *subdue* the fear of reaching out, because you need other people in order to overcome and succeed.

Pastors, licensed therapists, mentors, life-coaches, professionals and God-fearing people; parents, relatives, seasoned achievers, trustworthy friends and neighbors; books, audio and visual media, and the internet are all potential *sources* for wise counsel. However, you must exercise *caution* and be willing to *examine* all the information to make sure it is in *agreement* with The Word of God.

God will always use people to *help* you, one way or the other. Just as one person can be an added *dilemma* to your problem, another can be a *solution* to your problem. Invest in *right* relationships and waste no time with wrong ones.

2. The Fear...of Failure

Maybe you are *struggling* with...*a fear of failing.*

The fear of failure is *real.* You are not sure anything you try will succeed, so you cling to your *reactionary* posture. Your plans are preconceived as dead-ends even before you give them a try. The inner promptings to make changes that could create good results are *dismissed* as quickly as you conceived them. They become a pile of statistics by which you catalogue your failures. As you do this, it adds to your sorrow and discouragement. Consequently, your fear of failure *mounts.*

Confront...the mountain.

A good way to do so is to *analyze* the cause of your problem and to face it *squarely.* Many have failed to pursue their dreams because of fear. Fear breeds fear which gives birth to the dreaded end result: failure!

3. The Fear…of Fear

Are you afraid…but not really sure what you are afraid of?

Are you unable to *admit* your fear to yourself? It is a fear…*of the unknown.* You are confused and somewhat unsure about what is *really* going on. You suspect that God may be *testing* you. You *languish* in your fear, believing that God is paying you special attention just like Job; and that He is not yet done with His experiment.

John 14:27; *"Peace I leave with you; My peace I give you. I do not give to you as the world gives. Do not let your heart be troubled and do not be afraid."*

The Bible acknowledges, *"Fear does not come from God because perfect love casts out fear."* (See 1 John 4:18.)

> *Just as a person can be a problem; a person can also be the solution to your problem.*

It is imperative that you learn to cast out fear.

Rid yourself of irrational fear because it is not from God. Fear *reproduces* like cancer…and only creates *more* fear; which is *self-defeating.*

5 Keys To Casting Out Fear

1. Casting Out Fear...By The Power of The Holy Spirit.

2 Timothy 1:7 NLT; *"For God has NOT given us a spirit of fear and timidity, but of power, love, and self-discipline."*

Isaiah 41:10 NASB; *"Do not fear, for I am with you; Do not anxiously look about you, for I am your God. I will strengthen you, surely I will help you, Surely I will uphold you with My righteous right hand."*

The Holy Spirit will always *warn* you of dangers ahead, either through silent talks, dreams, other people or the things around you. You can operate on a new and higher level when you become *aware* of the tricks and plots of the enemy through *revelation* from The Holy Spirit.

2. Casting Out Fear...By The Word of God

Matthew 11:28; *"Come to Me, all you who are weary and burdened, and I will give you rest."*

Research on and study what The Word has to say pertaining to fear, and of course *courage*; which is the opposite of fear. What if you were *guaranteed* a victory *before* you ever went into a battle? Would that *increase* your confidence level? That is exactly how life is for those who *believe*, *trust* and *obey* God. In Matthew 28:18, Jesus Himself assured His disciples, *"All authority in earth and on heaven has been given to Me."*

You cannot go wrong by *pleading* The Blood of Jesus over your life and your circumstances. The Blood of Jesus is to evil forces what *insecticide* is to bugs!

3. Casting Out Fear...By The Use of Affirmations

1 Cor 2:16; *"… But we have the mind of Christ."*

The use of self-affirmations *builds* self-confidence like nothing else does. Dr. Harold Herring of the Debt Free Army often references how powerful it is to personalize the scriptures with your own name. You can and should be saying aloud to yourself: *"I will overcome, I am a conqueror, I have the mind of Christ, and greater is He that is in me than he that is in the world."*

You can also overcome fear by constantly assuring yourself that God is *with* you, not against you. God is your *Ally* not your enemy. Your situation is not permanent...*only temporary*. Every trial has an *expiration* date, if you don't quit *prematurely*. Jesus *lightens* your burdens. In Matthew 11:30, He declares, *"For My yoke is easy and My burden is light."*

4. Casting Out Fear...By The Knowledge of Other Victors

History is full of great *achievers*, dead and living alike, who have *overcome* painful experiences and gone on to achieve dreams of paramount importance.

Dr. Mike Murdock often encourages *reading* the life stories of people whose lives we *admire*. By the same token, I urge you to do the same. You will discover that the chapters of their lives are indeed a *collection* of their experiences. You will not only be encouraged by the things they went through and overcame, but more importantly, you will *appreciate* God's plans for your life even more.

Your discoveries from studying others will *uncover* a new awareness that you are not *alone* in your struggles. It gives a new perspective to your journey as a *corporate* battle instead of as a *lonely* burden.

Word of Caution

The *acknowledgement* of the trials and challenges you face must not be mistaken as an invitation to *settle* for a life of *perpet-*

ual endurance of rough times without relief. You do not have to live your life *tolerating* constant suffering.

To view adversity strictly as an *inevitable* burden or a *necessary* evil can lead to an attitude of concession to situations that must be *changed* or even *resisted*. There should be no special tolerance for hardship as a part of the God-life.

Chapter 3

Battle Dos...And Don'ts

There are differences in people.

These differences show up in the way we *respond* to situations. For some, adversity is a *wake-up* call. Such people usually move *quickly* into action without delay when crises arise.

There are others who would not do anything unless somebody *appeases* them or perhaps something *pushes* them into action.

Then, there is a third group who would rather *die* with the problem or hope the problem dies *before* they can take action. Such people resort to what psychologists have termed "learned helplessness," a situation in which one *gives up* trying under the erroneous assumption that their situation is *unchangeable*. Such individuals perhaps bet *against* their circumstances to test who between them has the most *staying* power.

To which of these three categories above do *you* belong?

It better not be the last one! Some people do nothing because they do not believe they can create any change in their circumstances, so their problem *lingers*. It is unreasonable for you to always do *nothing*. Just imagine two boxers in the ring, where one is *motionless* and does nothing but takes punches. Very soon he or she would drop down in a heap. That is what you do when you do not fight back.

During my basic training in the Army, I witnessed a reaction that has never left me. A Platoon Sergeant had become *infuriated* with a Private who had *refused* to utter a word in *response* to his admonition. He made the statement, "I would prefer you tell me to eat *sh*** or something than to keep mute."

I ask for your forgiveness in not filtering out the profanity, but the purpose is for you to appreciate that you *have* to fight back in some way in order to *disable* your oppressor. Only then are you *able* to take the power *away* from them.

Silence can also be a very powerful tool...especially when it is the *appropriate* weapon for your situation.

You have a conglomeration of options on what to do when your life is under any kind of assault; whether *physical, emotional* or *spiritual.* Here are some simple and quick reactions you can make.

...*Ask* for help or guidance from The Holy Spirit.

...*Say* something.

...*Pray* in the spirit.

...*Scream* The Name "Jesus!"

...*Pray* with authority in The Name of Jesus.

...*Ask* questions.

...*Speak* to your situation.

...*Talk* to someone.

...*Run* to safety.

Fight back...in some way instead of doing nothing or giving up. You neither want to be your enemy's *punching bag;* nor enjoy being a *victim* of your circumstances.

Remember This…During A Season of Trial

Warfare must be *resisted*…not *tolerated*.

Warfare may be *inevitable*…but it is not *undefeatable*.

There are *hidden lessons* behind every test and trial intended for your *knowledge, growth* and *development* or the *discovery* of the high calling of God in your life. Do you remember what I shared earlier in the book? My own afflictions helped me *discover* prayer like never before and out of that experience we became "Prayer Warriors."

Adversity is not *necessarily* something from God, intended to *test* your endurance. So *arm yourself properly* with The Word of God and fight back.

Your mountain is not *insurmountable*. Others have climbed even *bigger* mountains with triumph, and so can you.

You must not *waver* in your faith, because *true* faith is trusting God when things do not seem to be going in your favor. You are not *alone* in your battle as we are reminded by the scripture:

1 John 4:4; *"But you belong to God, my dear children. You have already won a victory over those people, because the Spirit Who lives in you is greater than the spirit who lives in the world."*

God Himself *knew* you would encounter storms and *promised* to see you through your difficult and lonely times:

Isaiah 43:2; *"When you pass through the waters, I will be with you; and when you pass through the rivers, they will not sweep over you. When you walk through the fire, you will not be burned; the flames will not set you ablaze."*

In The Midst of Affliction, Never...

1. Abandon Your Bible

There may not be a *generic* solution to the distinct challenges you will face and experience in your personal struggles. However, to the believer, The Bible remains the *common* denominator and the blueprint for *scriptural* solutions to problems. Read and meditate on The Word *daily*. You do not have to read a *whole* chapter if the thought of doing so feels overwhelming to you. Just start from somewhere. *Meditate* on whatever stands out to you.

2. Get Angry With God

God might have *permitted* your situation but He did not *create* it! Do not *misplace* your anger. Do not get mad at The One Who has the *solution*; rather get mad at *the source* of the problem. Get mad at the devil, at your polluted mindset; *but never at God.*

3. Get Mad At People

Your boss, spouse, children, relatives, pastor, teacher, mentor, and friends alike are not to blame. There may be a person or people involved with the creation of your problem, but be careful to *target* your anger appropriately.

Never go on a *blaming* spree.

If you wage the *wrong* war, you could *complicate* your problem and *prolong* your adversity. This is not time to tell your boss how wrong he or she is and how right you are. If you do, you *both* stand to lose.

Carefully *choose* your battles. Avoid those who *drag* you down. Stay close to those who *lift* you up.

4. Hold Grudges

You cannot wage warfare successfully without *letting go* of past hurt. You must *forgive* yourself and others who have wronged you. *Free* yourself. God cannot work with you while you refuse to let go of your emotional baggage...past disappointments and past hurts.

Mark 11:25; *"And when you stand praying, if you hold anything against anyone, forgive them, so that your Father in heaven may forgive you your sins."*

5. Divide Your Focus

Choose your focus no matter how *farfetched* the end result may seem. Learn to *protect* your focus. Traveling on a *wrong* road could be *costly*. An African proverb says, "A dog that chases two prey simultaneously does not make a kill."

Maintaining your focus can be very *hard* and even *confusing* at times; more so in *dire* situations. Yet, focus is an *indispensable* tool for your *success* and *liberation*. Identify what truly matters and give it your *undivided* attention. What truly *matters* is not necessarily what consumes your thoughts. Isolate what truly matters, from the thing that *shatters*.

Philippians 3:14; *"I press on to reach the end of the race and receive the heavenly prize for which God, through Christ Jesus, is calling us."*

6. Become Tied To Your Comfort Zones

A time of *adversity* is a time of *battle*. Do not *settle*. Do not *restrain* yourself to your comfort zones. For example, are you doing things the *same* old way because that is *easier*? Are you really expecting a *different* result? Or maybe you are after a *temporary* fix? Like going to the mall on a shopping spree or leaving town for a gateway; just to find *arbitrary* relief to your discomfort. That may seem soothing, but it is only temporary and oftentimes *misleading*.

Avoid places of *entrapment* that may seem *comforting*, but have no real connection to your goals. Several of the clients I counseled have shared with me how they ended up in *serious* legal and financial trouble by trying to escape from their problems. The exception to the rule is *only* when you are *prompted* by The Voice of God!

A better alternative to pursuing a temporary fix would be to *stay close* to your mentors, become *active* in your church and *surround* yourself with people capable of motivating, empowering and steering you in the *right* direction.

7. Take Unnecessary Risks.

Do not permit *trivial* risks during your storms.

...*Trusting* and *confiding* in others too soon.

....*Speeding* and wishing you would not get a ticket.

...Letting *anger* take control of situations.

...Making *impulsive* decisions.

...Walking away from your job in *exasperation* because your boss aggravates you.

...*Talking without thinking* things through; more so since you cannot take back your words once they have been uttered.

Stupid risks could be *simple* and *easy* to make; but their costs are *high*. I liken taking such risks to *freely* giving your adversary a pair of handcuffs and all the keys that come with it, then *willingly* putting your hands behind your back for him/her to restrain you. Imagine getting a speeding ticket and trying to pay it off when you are flat broke?

8. Quit Or Give Up

You cannot win by doing *nothing*.

Remember the analogy of the boxer who stares at his opponent without any *defensive* movement, punches or jabs? Wouldn't the opponent knock him down and out in a matter of minutes? That is what you are doing when you lay on the couch all day, *hoping* your problem would go away.

When you go to bed at night and wake up each morning without praying, you are *giving* the devil the upper hand.

Proverbs 24:10 ESV; *"If you faint in the day of adversity, your strength is small."*

14 Keys To Navigating Through Adversity

1. Continuously *evoke* The Word of The Living God; *believing* and *reminding* God of His promises through His Word.

2. *Assess* your situation to determine *the source* of your problem. If your sink is *overflowing*, would it not make sense to turn the water off *first* before trying to *mop* the floor?

3. Constantly *encourage* yourself no matter how dire the situation appears. Take advantage of the power of *your words*. Speak *positive* things to yourself, no matter how hard it may be. There is *power* in what you say.

Proverbs 18:21; "The tongue has the power of life and death."

4. Your next move will require proper *planning*, *order* and *organization*. If you have not already done so, *initiate* steps that will help you keep your life in check. Start today to *examine* your *spending habits*...both of your *time* and of your *money*.

5. Establish effective ways to *store* and *retrieve* information.

6. Learn to *plan* and *follow through* with your plans. If not, disorder will make the already bitter pills much harder to swallow. I am talking from experience!

7. Constantly *remind* yourself of the rewards of *overcoming* as revealed in the Book of Revelation, Chapters 2 and 3.

8. Embrace *Ephesians 6:10-18*...scriptural solutions to problems and develop the attitude, "winning is my only option."

9. *Strengthen* your *faith* and solidify your *trust* in God. *Remind* yourself that God cannot lie and always comes through on His promises.

10. Become a *rebel* to the forces of darkness by doing what nauseates the devil: continuously *thanking, pleasing, praising* and *uplifting* God both in good and bad times. Remind the devil that "two cannot walk together unless they agree." (See Amos 3:3). God is *The Source* of your blessings, not the devil.

11. Resolve to stay in *motion,* not *stagnation.* God once spoke to me during my drought season to "stay in movement," meaning to reach out to *people* and *places* and not attempt to die in the *silence* of my home. Doing so led to new *discoveries* and opened doors of *opportunities.* What had seemed so difficult suddenly became easy!

12. Continue *casting* your net. Expect a *bigger* catch.

13. Remind satan that he is a liar. Remember, God can neither *lie* nor *fail.*

14. *Forgive.* Forgiveness will *free* you from the bondage of past *painful* experiences.

Nelson Mandela is attributed with the saying, "Unforgiveness is like drinking poison and expecting another to die from it."

If there is any need to forgive, forgive today without delay. If you do not know *how* to forgive, *learn*. Forgiveness will *erase* the footprints and scars of past wrongs and reposition you for God's healing. Failure to do so will invite *depression* and the *blaming* of other people for your problems.

The blame game will *rob* you of the opportunity to take ownership of your situation. It will *deprive* you of God's empowerment for steering you into a new season. The scriptures abound with biblical teachings and commands to forgive. Luke 17:3 ESV; *"If your brother sins, rebuke him, and if he repents, forgive him."*

What You Can Expect In Following These Steps

You will begin to feel *empowered*.

Just imagine being able to *defeat* someone you were *afraid* of? When I was just 8 years old, I *fought* a bully who was *bigger* than me. My thought after that fight was, "I could have done this sooner."

You will move from the position of "I can't" to "I sure can!" You will begin to *release* your faith like never before and to *solidify* your trust in God; which *propels* you to action.

You will begin to *conquer* your own *self* and your *fears*.

When you have *conquered* fear...you are ready to face your *giants*. With every *victory*...your *confidence* increases. A higher level of confidence brings with it a *new posture*; the posture of a *warrior*. *Victor* instead of victim. You are now more adequately prepared to conquer in the many inevitable battles you will face in life.

4 Secrets To Demoralizing & Overcoming Enemy Forces

1. Testimony: You *overcome* through testimony.

Rev 12:11 NLT; *"And they have defeated him by The Blood of The Lamb and by their testimony. And they did not love their lives so much that they were afraid to die."*

Testify about the goodness of God in your life. Do not keep it a secret. Take a trip down memory lane and *recount* all the good things in your life. When you *talk* about the blessings of The Lord in your life, even during your seasons of affliction, the enemy feels *discouraged*.

1 Thess 5:18 NLT; *"Give thanks in all circumstances."*

2. The Blood of Jesus: You overcome by *pleading* The Blood of Jesus. The Blood was not shed in vain. Jesus paid the *highest* price. Plead The Precious Blood of Jesus on a *daily* basis; over your *life*...your *family*...your *finances*...your *marriage*...your *job*...your *health*...and just about *every area* of your life.

Satan cannot stand it. Your adversaries will know you are not an easy target. Do this...not once or twice; but as often as possible...*every day of your life*.

You may ask, "Why daily?"

Your adversaries have not ceased; they do not attack *once* and *stop*. Therefore, you have to be consistently *persistent* in your counteraction. Remember the saying, "Life is like riding a bicycle; you fall if you stop pedaling?"

When I was growing up, I used to think that once a man of God lays his hands on you and prays for you, that you would not have any more attacks. I have since learned the hard way. You cannot rely solely on the prayers of others, believing that they will sustain you for life. It is not enough for others to pray for you...*you must learn to pray yourself.*

Take authority by *continually* pleading The Blood of Jesus over your life.

3. Being Right With God: You overcome by living a life of righteousness. You cannot overcome if you live like the ones who are after you.

Think no evil *thoughts* and perform no evil *acts.*

Submit *fully* and *wholly* unto God, to the lawful authority over you, and most importantly to the power, guidance and direction of The Holy Spirit. You are not righteous, but you can live a righteous life by *pleasing* God. A life of righteousness breeds an aura of *protection* 24/7.

1 Thessalonians 5:22; *"Reject every kind of evil."*

4. Fulfilling Your Duties And Obligations: Fulfill your duties and obligations with *excellence.* If you perform in every situation "as if" you are being *watched* and *evaluated,* because more often than not you are; then you will come out a winner.

Why? Because, your enemies will have nothing *tangible* to hold *against* you. Evil people will find no evil to associate with your name. Good people will find no reason to be against you; if anything, credible reasons to be on your side. God will find you *attractive* for promotion.

Promotion is a *proof* of overcoming.

When you are promoted, you are now operating at a much *higher* level than the enemies who could not stop you. You have now entered a new realm of victory with a better and closer relationship to God.

If you perform in every situation 'as if' you are being watched and evaluated, your enemies will have nothing tangible to hold against you. Evil people will find no evil to associate with your name. Good people will find no reason to be against you and credible reasons to favor you. God will find you attractive for promotion.

Protect Your Momentum

A good starting point is to *reawaken* your interest in God's Word. Before God can start working with you in profound and supernatural ways, you must *master* His Word effectively.

You might say, "I have read certain Bible verses over and over while in my desperate zones but nothing happened."

I do not know a specific answer to your individual situation, but I do know what it cannot be. It cannot be because God's Word failed.

God's Word cannot fail.

God's Word Is His Will...And His Will Is His Word

Isaiah 55:11; *"As the rain and the snow come down from heaven, and do not return to it without watering the earth and making it bud and flourish, so that it yields seeds for the sower and bread for the eater, so is My word that goes out from My mouth. It will not return to Me empty, but will accomplish what I desire and achieve the purpose for which I sent it."*

There may be a number of untold reasons why reading The Word has not made a *significant* impact during your crisis.

Of course, the mere reading of The Word does not produce any *desired* change. Doing what it says is what makes the difference.

The Word of God is The Law of God.

The Law reacts in similar ways when it is *properly* applied, regardless of who applies it. It is possible you have no *direct revelation* of The Word from The Holy Spirit on your *specific* problem. Never *cease* or *lose* hope.

When The Holy Spirit is The One *directing* you, you will have a different *understanding* of the same Bible verses you may have read over and over before. With The Holy Spirit's guidance comes a *renewed* understanding...which initiates a new *effect* from God's Word.

Maybe you have been entertaining *doubt* at the same time you were seeking *scriptural* solutions. Doubt and faith do not work together. Doubt *paralyzes* you just as faith *births* miracles in your life. Doubt is to a miracle what water is to a fire!

When you have done everything you *can* and everything you *know* to do and your mountain still *refuses* to move, that does not mean that it is time to *quit*. If you *quit*, your miracle will be *aborted* and you will *lose* the prize of overcoming as promised in Revelation 3:12, 21.

I urge you to *keep believing.*

I implore you to *"stay in movement."*

I heard a man of God give the instruction "to walk around your mountain" if your mountain *refuses* to move. Walk around your mountain until you can *find* your bearing again.

In Hebrews 13:5, God promised, *"He will neither forsake nor abandon you."*

Living In Courage

Find encouragement through God's Word.

Always operate in courage. If you do not, your burden of discouragement will become too *heavy*. You may be down, but you are not out. The fact that you are not yet defeated means God's Word is still working for you. He is still protecting you from the enemy "who comes to steal, to kill and to destroy." (See John 10:10.)

It is important for you to understand the *efficacy* and *unlimited power* of God's Word. Constantly *assure* yourself that "if God is with you, no one can be against you." (See Romans 8:31.)

God is not *neutral* toward you or *against* you.

Keep *throwing power punches* and your opponent will soon come down in a heap. Keep *casting your net* and you will soon make your *biggest* catch ever.

What Is Your Victory-Formula?

Should you *formulate* a victory-equation for *every* battle?

Any act that produces a *desired* result will tend to be *repeated*. Are you able to *pinpoint* what made the difference in your *past* successes and victories without guesswork or doubt?

If you are a believer, The Holy Spirit can never be left out of your victory-equation or success-plan. He is *omniscient*. He cannot be wrong. Complete *confidence* and *trust* in Him, no matter what is going on in the world around you, will produce *desired* results. He will always come through at the *right* time.

Pastor Kenneth Davis often says, "The Holy Spirit may not be there when you want Him, but He will be there at the right time because He is an on-time God. His ways are different from our ways. He comes through for His true companions because He is faithful, reliable and trustworthy."

The question is: *Are you a true companion of The Holy Spirit? If not, what would it take?*

Caution: For Believers Only!

As a believer, I *struggled* accepting that God's promises in His Word were for *everyone*. I still vividly remember having this internal conversation. "This whole thing comes by selection, maybe for those with Jewish roots..." A day or two later, it was as if God answered me through a preacher that I heard on the radio while I was driving.

He said (paraphrased), "God's Word is like going to the gym. It works if you work it..."

Instantly, this thought hit me, "Yes, people who go to the gym get different results based on what they put into it."

My dear friend, God's Word is the same way. It works for those who believe. I could not find a better comparison.

Amos 3:3 KJV; *"Can two walk together, except they be agreed?"* You must *believe* God and His principles. *Surrender* your frames of reference, your human logic and doubts to The One Who created the universe.

You have probably never travelled to *all* the states or provinces in your *own* country. Imagine for a moment, how big our God is...*The Author and Architect of ALL Creation*. We oftentimes believe scientists when they tell us the amazing stories of how vast the universe is...yet we have hard time *believing* the promises of The One who *made* that universe.

Just *believe* God with *all* your heart and *do* what He *commands* through His Word, as you would your boss or supervisor. You cannot *truly* believe The Bible without believing *in* Christ Jesus. Yes, you must *first* make a decision for Jesus and believe that He died for you, if you have not done so already.

Give your life to Jesus and *believe* that you are saved because of the price He *paid* on The Cross. (See John 3:16.)

What If The Word Does Not Apply In My Situation?

If The Word of God will not work for you, *what* will?

If the Power of God will not protect you, *whose* will?

"If God be for you who can be against you?"

If The Word of God will not work for you, what will?
If the Power of God will not protect you, whose will?

Our Prayer Together

Dear Lord, I thank You for my consciousness. I am a proof of Your existence. I exist because You created me. Thank You for Your Word, and for sending Jesus Christ to die on The Cross for my sins.

Lord Jesus, I welcome You into my life today as I open the door of my heart to You and accept You as my personal Lord and Savior. I surrender myself wholly unto You.

I withhold nothing back as I let go of all my worries, fears, doubts and unbelief. I nail to The Cross my afflictions, sickness, poverty, disease, ignorance and any inherited curses that may be transmitting through my ancestry line.

I surrender them all and withhold nothing back. I thank You Lord for accepting me into Your awesome family which I have become a part of today as I accept Jesus as my personal Lord and Savior, Amen!

Chapter 4

Assembling Your Personal Battle-Toolkit

Your toolkit will not be built in a day.

Start building a toolkit of what to carry with you to "service calls." The tools that you put in your toolbox must not only be familiar to you, but *operable* and *reliable*. A *plumber* or *handyman* knows what *tools* to take to a service call. A *surgeon* knows what *instruments* he needs on the operating table. A *professor* knows his *curriculum* and what reading material to recommend to his students.

Every battle will require a *strategy* and *plan*. As a believer, do you *know* your indispensable tools with which to fight principalities and evil powers?

Ephesians 6:12 NLT; *"For we are not fighting against flesh-and-blood enemies, but against evil rulers and authorities of the unseen world, against mighty powers in this dark world, and against evil spirits in the heavenly places."*

The *best* electrician *without* the right tools may have a *problem* solving even a minor electrical issue. Conversely, another who may have the best *tools* at his disposal, but lacks *training*, will not be successful in resolving even the *simplest* malfunction.

The efficacy however, does not rest in the tools per se but on the *irrevocable* Power of God's Word. Not knowing *how* to operate certain equipment does not make the equipment *faulty*. It may seem like it is, causing the *ignorant* and the *untrained* to draw *faulty* conclusions, but that does not change the fact of the matter. The same is true for many who walk the path of Christianity. It is not enough to *know* God; you must understand *how* God operates. You must have His principles on how to *conquer* and *overcome* at your disposal.

Despite the uniqueness of your situation, your personality traits or background, you will need a *planned* solution to the many problems that confront you.

5 Indispensable Tools For An Overcoming Life

1. God's Word – *Know* God's Word.

Knowing God's Word is so important that I have *repeatedly* referenced it in this book to the point of redundancy. Have your Bible readily *available* and *accessible* so you can *remind* yourself and others what The Word says.

Aren't you thankful we live in an era of information explosion? Nearly *anyone* with the desire can have *instant* access to the scriptures through several means including the Internet, apps and other portable devices.

Believe what God has spoken through His Word. Declare it *boldly* over your life. The Word is a *weapon*. Be *conversant* with the scriptures that apply to your unique situations.

Make time for *communion* with The Holy Spirit. Pray in your heavenly language or tongues *daily*. Satan and his agents *dread* this. They cannot stand an atmosphere of praise and worship!

2. A Doubt-Free Mind - *Eliminate* doubt.

No matter what mountain you are facing make no room for doubt. Doubt or unbelief gives room to fear. Continuously *refocus* your mind on your *strengths*...not weaknesses, *victory*...not defeat, *advantages*...not disadvantages.

Instead of nurturing doubt, replace such thoughts with faith affirmations: *"I can do everything through Christ, Who gives me strength,"* (Philippians 4:13 NLT).

You stand to lose *nothing* by choosing *faith*; but *everything* by choosing *doubt*. Keep your mind in check. Know when you are *slipping* into a mindset of doubt. Learn *how* to get rid of doubt by substituting the negative with the positive...*fear with faith*. Doubt is a *poisonous* weapon from the enemy.

3. Revelation – Divine *insight*.

What has God *specifically* revealed to you? Whatever God has *spoken* will surely come to pass...but *only* if you *cooperate* and stay in *obedience*. Let God's promises *excite* and *energize* you.

I have been guilty of not getting excited and energized over God's promises. It seemed like I was waiting *endlessly* for "Thy Kingdom come." Then I learned *how* to add my faith to God's Word. His promises will not *materialize* out of the blue or fall in your backyard like manna from heaven. You must *activate* them in your life by *believing* and *reaching*.

Remembering God's prophesies over your life is an important tool that goes in your toolkit. Remember the stories about: Joseph's dream and his triumph over slavery; Abraham who had a picture of the stars; Gideon and God's Word to him, "thou mighty man of valor;" and Jeremiah's divine endorsement, "I made you a prophet while you were in the belly..."

Not one of these men *forgot* what God had spoken to them during their *drought* seasons. In fact, each man's *reality* was in direct *contradiction* to God's promises; but the promises came to pass because they *believed* God. He is a God of *fulfillment*.

Know what to *expect* based on God's revelation to you.

Reject and *resist* anything contrary.

4. Instructions – Divine *direction*.

What instructions has God given you? Are you able to *discover*, *understand* and *carry out* God's individualized instructions in your life? If you are doing what He assigned you to, then do not be afraid! If you have no specific instructions, start with the *general* rules. God often moves from general to specific, just as you cannot become a Pope without first being a catholic.

Scan your life for any instruction from God...whether *forgotten* or *ignored*. Follow through judiciously without alteration or negotiation. Some of them will require a *long* learning curve. If *God* instructed it, it can be *accomplished*. God's instructions should dictate your *focus*, *purpose*, and *assignment*. They are *critical* tools in the toolbox of an overcomer.

5. God's Reputation – Divine *ways*.

Are you able to *understand* God's modus operandi?

Can you *believe* beyond a shadow of a doubt that God cannot fail on His promises...regardless of your emotions and circumstances?

Numbers 23:19; *"God is not human, that He should lie, not a human being, that He should change His mind. Does He speak and then not act? Does He promise and not fulfill?"*

If you still *struggle* believing this, keep *building* your faith by *reading* the testimonies of others. Doing so will *re-ignite* your faith.

What Do All These Tools Mean?

As you may have noticed, the *first* of the five tools in your kit is something *physical* and tangible...while the rest are all *mental* and intangible.

This is in line with the teaching, "If you can succeed in your *mind* you can succeed in real *life*." If you *fail* in your mind your chances of success in real world are *slim*. Dr. Mike Murdock crafted this more appropriately through one of his famous quotations, "The battle of life is for your mind."

Remind yourself, God is a *Deliverer* of His promises.

The psalmist wrote, "His love never fails," (See Psalm 136:1) of which we are personally reminded through the inspiring song by "The Newsboys."

How Heavy...Is Your Burden?

The *challenges* you face will *test* your character. But "that too shall come to pass" if you do not *succumb* to the power and persecution of your adversaries. Your victory will truly begin in your mind.

Our Prayer Together

Lord, we thank You for being our Place of Safety and Refuge in times of turbulence, storms and stress. Thank You for relieving us of our heavy loads and burdens as we lay them permanently at the feet of Jesus; The One Who can handle them better. Amen.

Chapter 5

Your Weapon...The Word

You will face spiritual battles.

What spiritual battles are you facing in your life *today*? What is your *success* plan? What *weapons* are you fighting with? What is your *strategy?*" Are your weapons a fit with your strategies?

The Word of God...Is A Weapon

Proverbs 24:6; *"You need guidance to wage war, and victory is won through many advisers."* Ephesians 6:12 KJV; *"For we wrestle not against flesh and blood, but against principalities, against powers..."* Ephesians 6:13 instructs us to, *"Put on the full armor of God."*

You cannot embark on a war successfully without knowing the *enemy* you are facing and of course, your *capability*. You cannot defeat your adversaries without devising a *clear* success plan. The war of *life* is not a war of *choice*. Your enemies will wage war against you at one point or another. Sometimes, it will be at your *weakest* moments.

The *day* of battle is not the time for *training* or *preparation*.

The *day* of battle is not even a day for *fasting*; neither is it a time for *murmuring*. "Is God not going to help me?" It is the time to *execute*. You should have been training and preparing already.

...*Fasting* periodically.

...*Praying* daily.

...*Singing* songs of praise.

...*Worshipping* The Lord with anointed music.

...*Studying* and *meditating* on The Word.

...*Returning* The Lord's *Tithe.*

...*Sowing* your Seed and Offering.

...*Expecting* a Harvest.

...*Living* in righteousness.

...*Knowing* what The Holy Spirit has been speaking to your heart.

It is a time to put on the *whole* armor of God.

Ephesians 6:10-18; "Finally, BE STRONG in the Lord and in the strength of His might. Put on the FULL ARMOR of God that you may be able to stand against the devil's schemes. For our struggle is not against flesh and blood, but against the rulers, against the authorities, against the powers of this dark world and against the spiritual forces of evil in the heavenly realms. Therefore put on the full armor of God, so that when the day of evil comes, you may be able to STAND your ground, and after you have done everything, to STAND. STAND FIRM then, with the belt of TRUTH buckled around your waist, with the breastplate of RIGHTEOUSNESS in place, and with your feet fitted with the readiness that comes from the gospel of PEACE. In addition to all this, take up the SHIELD OF FAITH, with which you can extinguish all the flaming arrows of the evil one. Take the HELMET OF SALVA-TION and the SWORD OF THE SPIRIT, which is the WORD OF GOD. And PRAY IN THE SPIRIT on all occasions with all kinds of prayers and requests. With this in mind, BE ALERT and always keep on praying for all The Lord's people."

Embrace the battlefield of life like the *soldier* of Christ that *you* are. The Bible made it clear that The Word of God is a weapon.

Get a hold of this secret: *The Word...is The Weapon!*

God *created* The Universe with His Word. He gave His Word to us in the form of The Bible. Develop a *love* for The Word of God. Make Bible study a *daily* habit.

Stay *close* to The House of The Lord. *Attend* church functions and Bible studies *regularly*. By doing so, you are *immersing* yourself in and *equipping* yourself with the things of God; thereby making it *difficult* for adversarial weapons to pierce your shield of faith!

In The Word, you find the authority which belongs to Christ Jesus. Matthew: 28:18; *"All authority in earth and in heaven has been given to Me."* God's Word has a track record of *victories*.

If God's Word is ephemeral or null and void, Christianity would have been a part of *forgotten* history. If The Word of God *lacked* power and authority, The Body of Christ...

...*believers*...

...*apostles*...

...*prophets*...

...*pastors*...

...*evangelists*...

...*teachers*...

...*followers* and *messengers* of Christ alike through the ages, would have been wiped off the face of the earth by untold deadly attacks and evil forces directed against Christianity and Christians.

Most *true* Christians do not *doubt* or *question* whether there is power in The Blood of Jesus or in The Word of God. The doubt is usually about whether "it will also work for me."

Take Cover!

Soldiers in battle take cover from incoming fire! People run to safety, away from hurricanes...*but not towards the storm.* So, when you are barricaded by life's tormenting storms, will you run *away* from a place of safety? Therefore, it makes sense to stay *close* to The Holy Spirit.

The Holy Spirit will *guide* you to *the place of safety.* He will *direct* you to your *"Rhema"* Word...*appropriate for your situation.* When you receive a *direct* Biblical message from The Holy Spirit, you will become much more *convinced* that God's Word will work for you as much as it would work for any other spiritual *heavy-weight* that you have personally known or heard about.

Dr. John Bosman once said, "You believe before you see, not see to believe." He was referring to faith in action and miracles. "God's miracles are for those who believe."

Matt 9:21 NLT; *"If I can just touch His robe, I will be healed."*

Jeremiah 29:11 NLT; *"For I know the plans I have for you,' declares the Lord, 'plans to prosper you and not to harm you, plans to give you hope and a future.'"*

The enemy you face is a con-artist and great at deception. *Deception* is your enemy's *strongest* weapon. When you are deceived you will be *disappointed*...you will become *discouraged.* When you are discouraged, you will begin to have *doubt.* Emotional *fatigue* will set in. That is the road satan wants you to travel on. The further down this road you go, the *nastier* the things you encounter will be.

Arm yourself with the scriptures.

If you recall, when Jesus was *tempted* by the devil, He *quoted* the scriptures each time. Satan never *doubted* God's Word. Jesus knew satan understands the *validity* and *Power* of God's Word. If Jesus resorted to The Word, what does that tell you?

The Word works!

James 4:7 NLT; *"So humble yourselves before God. Resist the devil, and he will flee from you."*

A Touch of Divine Encouragement

1 Peter 5:8 NLT; *"Stay alert! Watch out for your great enemy, the devil. He prowls around like a roaring lion, looking for someone to devour."*

Psalm 144:1 NLT; *"A psalm of David. Praise the LORD, Who is my Rock. He trains my hands for war and gives my fingers skill for battle."*

Isaiah 54:17 NASB; *"No weapon that is formed against you will prosper; and every tongue that accuses you in judgment you will condemn. This is the heritage of the servants of the Lord, and their vindication is from Me"* so declares the Lord.

Job 13:15 NLT; *"God might kill me, but I have no other hope. I am going to argue my case with Him."*

Psalm 40:5; *"Many, Lord my God, are the wonders you have done, the things you planned for us. None can compare with You; were I to speak and tell of your deeds, they would be too many to declare."*

Psalm 35:27 NASB; *"Let them shout for joy and rejoice, who favor My vindication; And let them say continually, the Lord be magnified, Who delights in the prosperity of His servant."*

1 Samuel 17:47; *"All those gathered here will know that it is not by sword or spear that the Lord saves; for the battle is the Lord's, and He will give all of you into our hands."*

Isaiah 43:2 NLT; *"When you go through deep waters, I will be with you. When you go through rivers of difficulty, you will not drown. When you walk through the fire of oppression, you will not be burned up; the flames will not consume you."*

Isaiah 55:11; *"So is the word that goes out from My mouth: it will not return to Me empty, but will accomplish what I desire and achieve the purpose for which I sent it."*

1 Peter 3:12 ISV; *"For The Lord watches the righteous, and He pays attention to their prayers. But the Lord opposes those who do wrong."*

Have you ever been questioned why we must continually face *attack* and *persecution*, while The Bible has all these *victorious* promises?

There has never been a promise to the contrary. The Bible never promised the *absence* of attack. The Bible never assured us of a life *devoid* of enemies and adversaries. However, the efficacy of The Bible is *reinforced* when we pass through the danger zones of life *unscathed*. Victories are *testimonials* for soul winning, and they *build* on the strength of our convictions, for those already in The Kingdom. The examples of Daniel in the *lions' den* and Shadrach, Meshach and Abednego in the *fiery furnace* are classic examples.

In the absence of persecution, what would there be for God to deliver His people from?

Yes, God Permits Attacks!

Tests and trials are *rarely* from God, but they serve some *useful* purposes for both God and man. Pastor Josh Gonzalez once stated, "God can sometimes put you through tests so you can see where you stand." According to Pastor Josh, tests are for *your own sake* as "they enable you to know if you pass or fail" during your trials.

Yes, God knows *the end from the beginning* but humans usually do not. The end results can become *reference* points for testimonies. We can learn from the courage as well as the mistakes of others.

Chapter 6

Your Weapon...Prayer

Prayer is a conversation.

Prayer is simply *communication* with God. Communication presupposes that when one party is speaking the other is listening! Prayer is neither a thought nor a feeling; but a *verbal expression.* If you could *perfect* the art of talking with God; sending and receiving uninterrupted messages to and from Him, could there be anything more powerful and rewarding?

I do not know a whole lot about Prayer but I do know one thing for sure: Prayer is a *good* thing! It is an *effective* weapon because it steers God into action. Prayer, therefore, is *power.* Prayer helps to *connect* us to God. Prayer *unlocks, heals, strengthens, comforts,* and *encourages.* Prayer *tears down* evil forces, and *restores* the good. Prayer *activates* the Power of God.

The devil and his agents *dread* a Prayer Warrior, but tread all over the domain of one who is *slack* in Prayer. Prayer is *important* and more *varied* than many of us really know. I have heard my own pastor talk about "Conversational Prayer."

He held the view that not many Christians pray a "conversational type prayer." This suggests that your prayers, more often than not, are a *one-way* communication with God. Talking to God with the *expectation* that He will grant your requests, yet never *waiting* for Him to speak to you in return.

Prayer is an important weapon, yet it is commonly *misunderstood, ignored, misused* or *misdirected*; thereby lacking in effectiveness. An example could be someone praying to *win* the lottery without even bothering to *purchase* a ticket. Instead, they *should* be asking God for opportunities to *earn* and *become* someone greater than they are right now. I must confess, I am that person; but I ask that you keep it to yourself for now! *(Disclaimer: I am not encouraging you to go out and purchase a lottery ticket, either.)*

When Your Prayers Go Unanswered...

God is neither *deaf* nor *insensitive*. He *hears you* every time you pray. Your motives and attitudes can sometimes become *roadblocks* to Answered Prayer.

At times, God may "deny" your requests for reasons best known to Him. At such times do not belabor yourself, but pray for God's will to be done since you do not see what God sees. At other times, God may say "it is not yet time" or "it is not due season." Your answers are not denied...*simply delayed.*

Sometimes, your wishes are *granted* and you are *happy* with the outcome. Other times, your requests are granted, but you do not receive them because you are *enslaved* and *limited* by your own perception and the environment to which you are accustomed. In such cases, you may be accepting lack due to *ignorance* and the *failure to reach out* to receive what God has already made available to you; not because He *declined* your requests.

More often than not, you have to reach out in order to receive. Continually *ask, seek* and *knock* without giving up prematurely.

The Danger of Aborted Prayer

In the *midst* of your affliction, or even at any other time, it is a gravely dangerous to *stop* or *slow* down in your Prayer Life. Doing so will *embolden* your adversary and *stop* you from tuning in to God's channels of abundance.

God hears you *every time* you pray.

69

What if He was *spasmodic in* responding to certain Prayer requests? How can you *receive* if you have no hope? How can you receive during your due season if you *abandoned* Prayer and expectation simply because you got weary of *waiting* on God?

> *Prayer is an important weapon yet it is commonly misunderstood, ignored or misused by many.*

You cannot intercede for one another if you *relinquish* Prayer. Even in your time of *affliction*, you can be an *instrument* of Prayer and Intercession for others. Job prayed for his friends during his most dire situation; and God delivered Job from his own troubles.

Job 42:10 NLT; "*When Job prayed for his friends, the LORD restored his fortunes. In fact, the LORD gave him twice as much as before!*"

Pray and intercede for others *constantly*. It is one of the *bridges* to overcoming during your own adversity.

My wife has often opined, "Bear in mind, you need not pray for someone whose need you can meet through what God has accorded you."

You can become a *channel* for the flow of God's blessings in other peoples' lives. More so, knowing that your good deeds *count* could be a powerful inspiration during rough times!

Dr Mike Murdock quoted Ephesians 6:8 in saying, "*Whatever we make happen for others, God will make happen for us.*"

Your Role During Prayer

Prayer is so important, Christ Himself prayed *often*. He even taught His followers and the masses *how* to pray. Unfortunately "Our Lord's Prayer" as taught by The Master of Prayer Himself is becoming *less* appreciated; gradually *fading* from the memory of many people today. If you think this is an exaggeration, just ask the *average* child in America to *recite* "The Lord's Prayer." I remember growing up in a society where *every* child of school age could recite "The Lord's Prayer."

Prayer, as a *Tool*, has different *purposes* and *manifestations*. You need to know the *purpose* for which you are praying. As a believer, you have to pray in the spirit. Use your *heavenly language* if you have one. Your home should be an environment of Prayer, *designated* and *consecrated* to create an atmosphere of interaction with The Holy Spirit. Make it a place that *attracts* the manifest Presence of The Holy Spirit.

Prayer is not a conversation you have with yourself. You do not have to whisper your prayer; except if you are in certain *restricted* environments. I remember my days in the military. There were times there would be dozens of us sleeping in a tent. In such cases I had to say my prayers *softly* out of respect for others' privacy.

You do not have to *murmur* when you pray. Speak *boldly* so that not only God, but even your adversaries can *hear* you!

Pray...

...*valiantly*...

...*clearly*...

...*specifically*...

...*confidently*.

71

Pray with the *attitude* of a *conqueror.*

Pray with the *mentality* of a *warrior,* especially when praying against attacks on your life or your loved ones.

Your Prayer must not lack in humility because you are petitioning The One Who is *higher than* and *above* all things; *The One with the power to grant your requests.*

Believe your Prayer has been *answered.* Express your *thankfulness* to God, believing He has *already* come through on your request.

The Importance of A Prayer-Ritual

A *prayer-less* Christian is like a soldier in the battlefield without any ammunition...*a toothless bulldog that barks but cannot bite.* Without Prayer, there is not a whole lot you can do to fight back or defeat your adversaries. You must learn to pray *habitually* and to pray the *right way* too.

To borrow my wife's analogy, "If you invited a very important guest to your home, keeping your house in order would be part of your preparations as the host. You do not wait until your guest arrives before you start cleaning, decorating or even start preparing meals."

Welcoming God in your midst is the same. You have to get your domain in *order.* I was taught to *consecrate* a place and time at home for meeting with God on a *daily* basis. Doing so was life changing for me and my family. It helped everyone to be *prepared* and to constantly be in *expectation.* When you do this, God Himself will schedule meeting with you on His calendar!

Sanctify that part of your home with an attitude of *humility* and *honor* unto The Holy Spirit and He will show up when you are ready!

Some would argue that *Prayer* is what brings us into the Presence of God, not the *atmosphere* or the *preparation* we put into it; especially if you are away from home without the luxury of *decorum* or *space*.

Your *preparation* is a way to demonstrate *dignity* toward God, relative to the time and space you are in. Even if you decide to *host* your special guest at their favorite restaurant instead of in your own home, some preparation has to be made. You will *pay* for the meal, the services and the atmosphere of the restaurant. At the end of the day, some preparation has been made. The point is, you must not sacrifice honor for contentment. Therefore, put your *best* into creating spatial *magnificence* for God.

6 Elements of Prayer You Must Never Overlook

1. **Pr**aise – Praise the Lord! *Sing* songs of praise to The Holy Spirit to usher in His Presence. *Thank God* for all the great things He has done for you. Show *appreciation* for His goodness, compassion and mercy.

Psalm 96:1 ESV; *"Oh sing to the Lord a new song; sing to the Lord, all the earth!"*

2. **Repent** – *Repent, confess* and *acknowledge* your sins before God. Ask Him to *cleanse* and *purge* you of all your impurities and iniquities that could be a *hindrance* to your Prayer.

Isaiah 59:2 (paraphrased); *"Sin separates man from God."*

3. **A**sk – *Ask, Seek,* and *Knock.* Ask of anything in His Name *until* the answer is *revealed.* Seek until you *find.* Knock until the door is *opened.* Do not stop or succumb to barriers that could *interfere* with any of these processes.

Sometimes we do not receive because we are not mindful that the command to "ASK" is a process that involves ALL the three actions *simultaneously*. We halt or abort the process in its tracks by giving up *prematurely*; by asking, seeking but not knocking or knocking, seeking and not asking until the results are received.

Discuss all your important matters with The Holy Spirit.

Ask Him to *show* you the truth and to *guide* all your decisions and actions in accordance with His will. Ask, but allow The Holy Spirit to *speak* to you.

Matthew 7:7; *"Ask and it will be given to you; seek and you will find; knock and the door will be opened to you."*

4. <u>Yield</u> – Yield to God by *allowing* Him to work on your problems. Believe He has *heard* your Prayer and that He will *honor* His Word. Do not *retain* the same burden without laying it down at the feet of The One with the answers.

Matthew 11:28 ISV; *"Come to Me, all of you who are weary and loaded down with burdens, and I will give you rest."*

5. <u>Edify</u> – *Enlighten* yourself with The Word of God. *Study*, *reflect* and *meditate* on His Word. *Do* what it says.

2 Timothy 2:15 NLT; *"Work hard so you can present yourself to God and receive His approval. Be a good worker, one who does not need to be ashamed and who correctly explains the word of truth."*

6. <u>Rejoice</u> – *Rejoice* and *celebrate* His participation in the affairs of your life.

Isaiah 9:3; *"You have enlarged the nation and increased their joy; they rejoice before You as people rejoice at the harvest, as warriors rejoice when dividing the plunder."*

Just as not praying on any given day creates a feeling of remorse for a believer, an *established* Prayer-Ritual creates a feeling of *joy*.

Just as not praying on any given day creates a feeling of remorse for a believer, an established Prayer-Ritual creates a feeling of joy.

Chapter 7

Your Weapon…Love

Love is a force.

John 3:16; *"For God so loved the world that He gave His One and Only Son, that whoever believes in Him shall not perish but have eternal life."*

My darling wife, Ngozi, crafted it so beautifully. "Love began when God gave His Son and His Son gave His Life. A *Lover* is a *Giver* and giving is a *choice.*"

Love encompasses *care, sacrifice,* and *hard work.*

1 John 4:16-18; *"And so we know and rely on the love God has for us. God is love. Whoever lives in love lives in God, and God in him. This is how love is made complete among us so that we will have confidence on the day of judgment: in this world we are like Jesus. There is no fear in love. But perfect love drives out fear, because fear has to do with punishment. The one who fears is not made perfect in love."*

> *"Love began when God gave His Son and His Son gave His own life."*

Love is a *powerful* weapon. According to scripture, Love provides God's *protection*. Love *dissolves* fear, and fear breeds in the absence of Love.

In times of adversity, the Love you *exude* will *rally* in your favor. It will be to you what CPR is to one having a heart attack!

We as humans do not *understand* the full power of Love because we cannot fully *comprehend* Love. It is one of the least understood subjects because it is the *hardest* to master. It involves enormous *sacrifices*.

Love is the most *divine* of all the virtues of life, yet it cannot be wholly apprehended without some form of sacrifice or loss. Anyone experiencing adversity has a lot to learn from Love. Complete or total subjugation is nearly *impossible*. Love *absorbs* all pressures.

Labor in Love to *understand* Love: Love of *God*, Love of *self*, Love of *people* and Love of *wisdom*. The Bible even talks about Love of your enemies...which simply means *you are unable to conquer without Love*.

> *Love is the most profound of all the virtues of life yet it cannot be fully comprehended without some sacrifice or loss.*

Our Prayer Together

Dear Lord, teach us the astonishing power of Love. Remove every polluting thought, belief-system, idea, value and perception that feeds into our Love-Reserve; that we may begin to see, feel, perceive and understand through Love-filled senses. That we may increase in Love and attract the blessings of God's Love, through our Lord and Savior, Jesus, Amen!

Chapter 8

Your Weapon...The Seed

The Seed...is a Beginning.

The realization that our *actions* have *consequences* is no longer an issue of disagreement, even among young people. We know that when you *break* a law, you face some *consequences*. Similarly, when a farmer *sows*, he looks forward to a *Harvest*.

Disagreements often emerge when this principle is applied to sowing Money-Seed into God's Kingdom and *expecting* to receive a Harvest back from God. If all our actions have consequences, it makes sense that Seed-sowing into God's work is no different.

What rewards can one expect who sows money, time, affection, respect, mercy, hospitality, and gifts into others? If you *invest* in something, is it *wrong* to expect a *profit* or *return on your investment*? What then disqualifies you from sowing into God's work and expecting a *hundred-fold* return from God as He promised in the scripture?

Galatians 6:7 KJV; *"Be not deceived; God is not mocked: for whatsoever a man soweth, that he will also reap."*

A time of *drought* can be very challenging, but it is not the time to *hold back* on sowing with expectation of a Harvest; a point constantly emphasized by my own pastor. It may be *tempting* to think there is no need to keep sowing since the Seeds do not seem to produce any desired Harvests.

Proverbs 11:24-25; *"One person gives freely, yet gains even more; another withholds unduly, but comes to poverty. A generous person will prosper; whoever refreshes others will be refreshed."*

You have to be careful not to *withhold* your Seed during *adverse* seasons or even *confuse* your Seed with your Harvest. It is a time, more than any other, to be more *conscious* of The Soil you sow into. Evaluate and *qualify* The Soil through guidance by The Holy Spirit. You can also qualify The Soil by *assessing* the mission and vision of your benefactor.

My own pastor has taught us to *target* our Seeds for *desired* Harvests. Harvests are *blessings* from God to those who sow into *good* ground. The results continue to *multiply* and *reproduce*, and that is how you know it is from God. My wife often says, "When God does one thing, it accomplishes many."

The last thing you need during your season of affliction is financial *dryness*. Poverty *plus* hard times equals *a living hell*. My commander in the Army used to tell us during his safety briefings, "Don't be that guy!"

Do not be that guy...who *refuses* to sow.

Do not be that guy...who *eats* his Seed.

Do not be that guy...who believes that poverty is a sign of *humility* before God.

How unreflective and narrow-minded you can become when you think along such lines.

> *Poverty plus hard times equals a living hell.*

What about the lives of Abraham, Jacob, Joseph, Job, David, Solomon, the Apostle Paul and all the people in the scriptures that The Lord *blessed* with abundance? What about Godly men in your own generation that have *prospered* in hard times through Biblical principles? They prosper because they *obey* God's Laws of sowing and reaping with expectation of blessings from God.

Be Authentic

If it is "money" you need, do not ask God for "peace of mind" instead. *Political correctness* should be the last thing you are worried about during your season of affliction. Your peace of mind comes from The Holy Spirit; not from money.

Avoid the temptation to appear *modest*, so as not to *offend* people who may hold a different viewpoint and your critics. The bad news is that your critics will be offended *anyway*...regardless of what you say or do.

Be direct in your requests before God.

If you are in need of money, *ask* for the opportunities to earn *a lot* of money. Do not twist your requests in order to *appease* the world. Instead, *pleasure* The One Who is your Source and Provider by *releasing* your faith for what you *really* want. (See Hebrews 11:6.)

Can you receive what you have *not* asked for? Do you expect to receive *apples* when you have only asked for *oranges?* (See Matthew 7:9-11.) Believe that He will *reward* "the desires of your heart." (See Psalm 37:4.) You do not have to *settle* for what you think society *wants* you to have.

Hebrews 11:6 ESV; *"He exists and...He rewards those who seek Him."*

In times of adversity, *boldly* ask God for what you want...*sincerely* and *truthfully*. It will be a *catalyst* for the heavens to release an *explosion* of blessings and opportunities over your life.

God's Blessings Are Biblical Promises

God's *blessings* and *provision* are Biblical as documented in Luke 6:38 and Mark 10:30-31, among others. In these two scriptures, God *promised* an *overflow* of blessings and a *hundredfold* return respectively.

In John 21:5, Jesus *instructed* His disciples *where* to fish to earn a living after they had toiled all night without meat in their nets. Similarly, in 2 Corinthians 9:11; *"You will be enriched in every way so that you can be generous on every occasion, and through us your generosity will result in thanksgiving to God."*

If God *abhors* the rich and wealthy, why did He orchestrate for Joseph of Arimathea, a well-to-do man, to be the *custodian* of the body of Jesus for burial following The Crucifixion? (See Mark 15:43-46.)

Strive to *untangle* your mind of any *false* doctrine that could be *hindering* your growth. It could manifest in the form of the belief, "Prosperity and God do not mix." Unfortunately, *most* of us grew up with that reasoning.

Getting rid of it could take more work than simply *serving* God. Getting rid of that *limiting* belief will *require* you to constantly *research* the scriptures to become well-informed. Sit at the feet of a *successful* mentor...someone blessed, transparent and godly; who *willingly shares* the secrets of God's blessings in their own life. No person I know of shares more openly the secrets of God's blessings in his life better than Dr. Mike Murdock.

The lack of money is an *unnecessary*, extra load as you journey through the many dark seasons of life. Christianity as a whole cannot *win* in the battle of life without Prosperity. Your attitude has to *reflect* the Biblical *truths* and not society's *fabricated* lies and expectations.

Conversely, there are also some people on the other extreme who cling to the belief that being a Christian *guarantees* God's Prosperity and Blessing without their own participation. Being a *Christian* does not guarantee *Prosperity* any more than simply being a *parent* guarantees having *successful* children.

> *Being a Christian does not guarantee Prosperity any more than being a parent would guarantee having successful children.*

You do not have to be *dismayed* by the recycled lies that have been told over and over again; such that what was originally *untrue* has now become *truth*. Having *enough* money to *accomplish* God's will is a weapon...*just like Prayer*.

No Compromises

In your season of adversity, never fall into the temptation of *compromise*. It will be *tempting* or *easy* to let loose of the standards; both Godly standards and the judicious laws of the land. Some of the decisions you have to make *each* day in your various roles could become overwhelming.

For example, if you are a parent, the burden of raising your child according to God's standards can become intolerably *heavy*. You have to go the *extra* mile to convince your teenage son and daughter that they do not have to *watch* the same movies that "other children" watch. They do not have to *listen* to the same kind of music that others listen to. They do not have to resort to *profanity* as they please just because other kids, who have *unrestricted* boundaries from their own parental figures, do the exact same thing.

If you are single, you may be facing *peer pressure*. You may be *tempted* to seek *outlets* in the wrong places such as the bars, clubs, and parties where alcohol and promiscuity are common-place. By doing so, you drag yourself into the danger zone of *entrapment.* You are giving the enemy a pair of handcuffs while tying your hands behind your back.

That is why the Christian life is no easy road per se. It can be very *enjoyable* if you train yourself to make the *best* of life through *right decisions.* Making the best of life will certainly re-quire the right actions and reactions that God *expects* in every situation. If you *endure* through that road to the end, it is full of *Everlasting Rewards.*

Hebrews 12:11 NLT, *"No discipline is enjoyable while it is happening--it's painful! But afterward there will be a peaceful harvest of right living for those who are trained in this way."*

> *Making the best of life certainly requires the right ac-tions and reactions that God expects in every situation.*

Chapter 9

Your Weapon...Praise & Worship

Worship is a posture before God.

How often are you in the *Worship Mode?* Are you able and ready to willingly *glorify* God during good and bad times; including times of serious adversity when you are *depleted* of the passion to pursue your God-given dreams and goals?

Take time *each day* to honor God through Praise and Worship. Do so from *the bottom* of your heart. "Sing to Him a new song," as commanded by the scripture. Bow to God in *honor* and offer Him *genuine* Praise. (See Psalm 96:1-13.)

Every morning, it has been a common practice for everyone in my household, from the youngest to the oldest, to lie *prostrate before God* in Thanksgiving and Praise. This was just *a family tradition*; not a religious ritual or obsession to salvage an ailing family. Praise *attracts* the Presence of The Holy Spirit and *repels* evil forces. Praise is so important to me that my *youngest* and *only* daughter is named Praise.

The devil cannot stand an *atmosphere* of Praise and Worship. You are the one who receives the *benefits* from Praise, because God remains the same whether we worship Him or not. We get blessed when we worship. Praise is really not for God's benefit...*but for ours.* In times of adversity, give God some *genuine* Praise!

Worship is a *gateway* out of the deep hole of adversity.

Chapter 10

Your Weapon...Tithes & Offerings

The Tithe is exclusively...The Lord's.

Are you returning The Lord's Tithe *regularly* and in a *timely* manner? Tithing is a *demonstration* of your *trust* in God. If you do not Tithe regularly, your mind will become *troubled* and *unsettled* during seasons of adversity. You will be *vacillating* in your faith and confidence instead of *focusing* your energy on seeking other solutions to your problem. You now have a *prime* suspect to worry about, *unpaid* Tithes; as the possible *cause* of your dilemma. You now have to *correct* that...and doing so *consumes* time and energy.

Withholding God's Tithe is *stealing* from God.

Malachi 3:8; *"Will a mere mortal rob God? Yet you rob Me. "But you ask, 'How are we robbing you?' "In Tithes and Offerings."*

Holding back The Tithe and your Offerings suggests you perceive giving as a *loss* or a mere *giveaway* instead of as Seed with *multiplying* potential. Tithing is a *divine command* with the *promise* of Rewards. God promises to *"Open the windows of heaven and pour out blessings that you will not have enough room to receive."* (See Malachi 3:10; Luke 6:38.)

Paying The Lord's Tithe *promptly* and *regularly* entitles you to God's *Promises* in return. Withholding The Tithe also has repercussions.

Malachi 3:9 NLT; *"You are under a curse, for your whole nation has been cheating Me."*

When you Tithe *habitually*, you can then *remind* God of His Promises...*particularly during your dry season*. Withholding The Tithe creates a punishing sense of *guilt* and a sinkhole of *regret*. You should not only Tithe *habitually*; but you must also give God the *best* of your fruits, just like Abel did. (See Genesis 4:4.)

I remember a time when my wife and I were so *broke* that we would Tithe with our credit card; because our paycheck was barely enough to cover all our expenses. Then one day, my dutiful wife said to me, "Maybe we are not giving God the best of our fruit by tithing from a credit card instead of from our earnings."

Instantly, an alarm went off in my head. I said to myself, "What an epiphany!" That day, we resolved to pay The Tithe *first* before spending and *never* to pay The Tithe from our credit card. The testimony from that is...all the bills were *paid on time* and we have *abolished* the credit cards!

We felt better afterwards knowing we are giving God *The Best*. We also increased in confidence *knowing* that God has not reneged on His Promises.

Chapter 11

Your Weapon...Right Relationships

Relationships matter.

You can neither succeed in *isolation*, nor can you engage in spiritual warfare *alone*. You need *alliances*...through *Right Relationships*.

Take advantage of the Prayer request invitations from *different* ministries. Form a *circle* of Prayer Partners so you can pray for one another. If your mother and father are people of faith, have them pray for you.

Unity of purpose is a *force*.

You need other people in your life to be your allies. Not only for Prayer and Intercession, but for *information-sharing, mentorship* and *friendship*. The question is, do you know who is *right* for you? What *qualities* should you look out for in a *friend* or a *mentor*?

Make a *list* of the attributes and qualities you are looking for in a friendship. If you observe those attributes and qualities in a person, that could be a *clue* for you to approach them. If on the other hand you observe the opposite of what you desire, that may also be a signal to exercise *caution*, to *avoid* them or even beat a hasty *retreat* as the situation dictates.

1 Corinthians 15:33; *"Do not be misled, 'Bad company corrupts good character.'"*

Where can you *find* quality people?

Are you a *member* of a local church? If so, that is *viable* ground. Church attendance does not *guarantee* they are a fit or worthy to be your desired friend, but that environment can serve as *qualifier*. Would you rather go to the bar at midnight and ask an intoxicated man with a glass of whiskey on one hand and a cigarette on the other if he would be your friend? You need a process of elimination to weed out those who do qualify for relationship...*those who do not line up with your values.*

Who Has Gone Through What You Are Going Through?

You need to *remind* yourself of well-known people of God, from the past and in the present, who have *experienced* and *conquered* challenges in their own lives.

In order to *ease* your weary mind, *remind* yourself that others have fought *similar* battles and emerged *victorious*. Think about an honorable person you know of today. Behind his or her glory, there was *a story*. I heard a preacher put it this way, "You know my glory but you do not know my story."

Revisit the lives of Joseph, David, Elijah, Elisha, Daniel, Jesus, the Apostles Peter, John and Paul; and many others in The Bible. *Reflect* on their profound lives. Is there any among them whose life was not wrapped in an adversity that they had to *overcome?*

Greatness can appear ready-made to the rest of us, but all achievers *endured* pain, suffering or loss of some kind to get to where they are. Every great achiever had to be *polished* before they could shine and glitter.

You are no different.

Chapter 12

Your Weapon...The Right Attitude

Attitude Affects Success.

What is your attitude towards God's Kingdom? Are you a part of a ministry by *support* or *active* engagement? Are you involved in *spreading* The Good News?

Luke 9:60 NLT; *"Let the spiritually dead bury their own dead! Your duty is to go and preach about the Kingdom of God."*

What is your attitude towards a *messenger* of God? Do you brand and paint God's ministers with *profane* brushes? Do you join in their undue criticism and crucifixion when they *fall* or make *mistakes*, even without all the facts other than what was portrayed in the media or through public opinion?

You cannot join the world in *crucifying* or issuing public rebuttals of a man of God no matter what you heard from other sources.

Why is this so important?

On countless occasions, many Christians who are *admirable* in their own right, have engaged in *undue* criticism and caricature of other ministers or ministries as if they are *their* adversaries. What you say *publicly* about a preacher or pastor should matter to you because it *matters* to God. They are God's messengers!

Such public castigation has *spiritual* implications. It can *deter* new people from entering The Kingdom. It can *stop* many from giving their lives to Christ, and others from committing to the works of ministry; because their minds have been *polluted* by your negative statements or opinion.

Would you expect *favorable* reactions or *quick* intervention from God if you are among those *sabotaging* Kingdom assignments? Kingdom-criticism encourages *seclusion* instead of inclusion or participation; yet we need *participation* if we expect to *fulfill* God's command to *spread* The Good News.

Hebrews 10:25; *"Not giving up meeting together, as some are in the habit of doing, but let us encourage one another."*

Are You A Part-Time Lover?

There are people who *remember* God only when they are in *dire* need of a miracle or favor. Others *seek* the assistance of ministers or churches only when they *need* prayer, intercession, child dedication, marriage rites, funeral rites, counseling, and so on.

There is nothing wrong with knowing *where* to seek help and reaching out for that help in times of need. My point is that nothing must *displace* the need for unwavering *commitment to* and consistent *participation in* the same ministries that serve our needs in good and bad times. If you do not believe in and honor a man of God in your *good* times, what makes you believe him in your time of *need?* How you *react* to God's *own* can influence how God reacts to *you.* During your season of adversity, consider your reactions. It could be a *gateway* to your new season of *Miracles.*

Our Prayer Together

Dear Lord, please help us to see others with Godly, not worldly lens and to judge charitably not critically, in The Name of Jesus.

Chapter 13

What Has God Called You To Do...In The Kingdom?

You have a Kingdom Assignment.

Proverbs 22:29 NLT; *"Do you see any truly competent workers? They will serve kings rather than working for ordinary people."*

What is your *Calling* in life? What has God called *you* to do? Are you even sure without a shred of doubt that you are operating at the *center* of your Calling? If you are not sure, you may want to find out. The reason is obvious; doing what you love *best* would not only help you to *be* at your best but it will also help you to *increase* in favor.

You can find out what your Calling is in several ways: through your *talents*...your *skills*...or your *passion*. You can also discover your Assignment through *revelation*, *reflection* or *research*. I highly recommend the book, *The Assignment*, by Dr. Mike Murdock.

When you *discover* your passion, God can begin to use you *more* than you ever imagined, just like He did Saul; who later became the Apostle Paul. In my opinion, he is the *greatest* missionary who ever lived after Christ.

During *turbulent* times, assess to see if there is a Calling on your life that you have *ignored* or not yet *discovered*. It could be the *vehicle* to the new future you desperately aspire. If you are at the *wrong* place and you *know* that for sure, then you need to summon the *courage* to make a *change*.

Someone said, "No matter how far you have travelled on the wrong road, it is best to turn back." More so, if you expect to reach your *desired* destination.

Any *effort* to discover your passion, talents and skills is a *worthwhile* investment since being in a *wrong* job or place adds an *extra* load to the weight you carry during turbulent times.

> *"No matter how far you have travelled on the wrong road, it is best to turn back if you must reach your destination."*

What To Do...When Nothing Seems Right

There may be times when you may have done *everything* you know to do but *nothing* seems to be going *right* for you. During such times, you become desperate for *tangible* results. When you reach the point where you can no longer *sustain* your hope and motivation, you *convince* yourself you are *justified* in quitting or suspending your efforts. However, that is in *contradiction* to the Biblical teaching of *faith* in *action*.

Micah 7:7, 8; *"But as for me, I watch in hope for the Lord, I wait for God my Savior; my God will hear me. Do not gloat over me my enemy! Though I have fallen, I will rise. Though I sit in darkness, the Lord will be my Light."*

Hebrews 11:6 NLT; *"And it is impossible to please God without faith. Anyone who wants to come to Him must believe that God exists and that He rewards those who sincerely seek Him."*

Faith in action...means *believing* when nothing seems right.

Tribulation will not only *test* your faith, it will *expose* the trajectory of your loyalty. Your loyalty is either towards God or away from Him...and there is no *middle* ground. When you have done all you can and nothing seems right, just remember that God is *always* right. When you have done all you can but still have no clue or explanation as to what *caused* your situation, just remind yourself that God has the answer.

While no one can fully *comprehend* God; those who know Him well understand that He can be *wholly* trusted because He *never* disappoints. Do not be tempted to tread the *broad* and *easy* path when God is showing you a different route.

Your last resort is to keep *believing* God *non-stop* and to keep *resisting* the devil *tirelessly.* Pray *daily.* Learn to stay *positive.* Try again and again...*without ceasing*...since doing nothing does not help either. Keep on pedaling the bicycle of life so you do not fall off. Sooner or later, your efforts will pay off.

Psalm 30:5 NLT; *"Weeping may last through the night, but joy comes with the morning."*

Pastor Kenneth Davis once opined, "Each time we go through the storm there will be some form of damage, and re-construction has to take place."

God is a *Finisher* and an active *Participant* in your *rebuilding* process. Just like He was with you at the beginning, He will see you through the end of it all.

God will not *abandon* or *forsake* you. (See Deuteronomy 31:6.) God will *restore* what the worms and locust have *devoured.* (See Joel 2:25).

Job 8:7 NLT; *"And though you started with little, you will end with much."*

Our Prayer Together

That your faith may remain steadfast and unshakable as you labor in God's vineyard and expect your crown of victory and glory! May you move from victory to victories and from glory to glories, through Christ Jesus, the Name above all names, Amen!

Will You Accept Jesus Christ As Your Lord & Savior Today?

If so, pray this short prayer according to Romans 10:13: "Whosoever shall call upon The Name of The Lord shall be saved."

"Lord Jesus, I believe in my heart that You are The Son of God. I believe that You died for my sins and were raised from the dead on the third day for my justification. I accept You this day, _____, as my Lord and Savior. I open my heart to You as I receive Your forgiveness, Your salvation and eternal life. From this day onward, let The Holy Spirit of God be my Guide. Confirm to me that I have received You, through Your Love, Peace, and Joy that can only come from knowing You; in Jesus' Name, Amen!"

If you would like to receive additional resources for new beginners in the faith or maybe you just need prayers or to share this important decision with us, simply let me know by stating:

☐ I made a decision for Christ today, _____

☐ Please keep me in your thoughts and prayer as you celebrate with me

☐ Send me additional resources

Email us at info@TheOvercomersToolkit.com

Visit our website: www.TheOvercomersToolkit.com

Partner With Us

Would you help make *daylight* out of somebody's darkness..? By ordering copies of *The Overcomer's Toolkit* and sending them as gifts to help others discover new ways of overcoming through Godly principles!

Yes, you can also partner with us by helping to make this book available to the less privileged and people of school age!

Special discounts are available for bulk-ordering of 10 or more copies of *The Overcomer's Toolkit.*

2 Ways To Order Your Copy:

1. Go to www.TheOvercomersToolkit.com

2. Email us at info@TheOvercomersToolkit.com

www.ingramcontent.com/pod-product-compliance
Lightning Source LLC
Chambersburg PA
CBHW070540030426
42337CB00016B/2282